GLOUCESTERSHIRE

Edited by Allison Dowse

First published in Great Britain in 2003 by
YOUNG WRITERS
Remus House,
Coltsfoot Drive,
Peterborough, PE2 9JX
Telephone (01733) 890066

All Rights Reserved

Copyright Contributors 2002

HB ISBN 0 75434 199 2
SB ISBN 0 75434 200 X

FOREWORD

This year, the Young Writers' The Write Stuff! competition proudly presents a showcase of the best poetic talent from over 40,000 up-and-coming writers nationwide.

Young Writers was established in 1991 and we are still successful, even in today's modern world, in promoting and encouraging the reading and writing of poetry.

The thought, effort, imagination and hard work put into each poem impressed us all, and once again, the task of selecting poems was a difficult one, but nevertheless, an enjoyable experience.

We hope you are as pleased as we are with the final selection and that you and your family continue to be entertained with *The Write Stuff! Gloucestershire* for many years to come.

CONTENTS

Belmont School (Area Special)
    Katie Johnson   1
    Hannah Lewis   1
    Richard White   2
    Charlotte Berry   2
    Tanya Wise   2
    Jamie Wright   3
    Daniel Kear   3
    Binyaameen Watson   3
    Aimee Kirby-Giles   4

Maidenhill School
    Lee Powell   4
    Jake Martin   5
    Sophie Prosser   6
    Christopher Budding   7
    Hannah Chivers   8
    Stacey Slocombe   8
    Toby Hinde   8
    Daniel McIntosh   9
    Holly Taylor   10
    Aaran Leach   10

Newent Community School
    Beth Sutton   11
    Hannorah Stephens   12
    Lauren Hobbs   12
    Siobhan Vye   13
    Stephanie Mowbray   14
    Lucy Ryan   14
    Vicky Howell   15
    Kate Richards   16

Rednock School

Gemma Louise Meyer	16
James Shelley	17
Lois Tucker	18
Joseph Dimery	18
Natalie Williams	19
Sophie Scott	20
Lizzie Burgin	20
Jenny Caesar	21
Rose Chard	22
Fergus Harris	22
Jenny Hoskins	23
Stephanie May	24
Benjamin Vick	25
Fiona Speak	26
Carly Hillier	26
Verity Everett	27
Danielle Smith	28
Chloe Williams	28
Richard Walton	29
Dora Meredith	30
Sara Price	31
Marcus Tibbitts	32
Jennifer Pedrick	33
Kim Blick	34
Becky Allen	35

Ribston Hall High School

Faiza Hadi	35
Natasha Frewer	36
Elizabeth Sheils	37
Nadia Tavana	38
Danielle Talbot	38
Laura Holdsworth	39
Heather Owen	39
Natalie Hall	40
Jodie Luce	41
Victoria Dovey	42

St Edward's School, Cheltenham
- Edward Bradley — 42
- Becky Taylor — 43
- Laura Tyler — 44
- Emma Jenkins — 45
- Helen Soutter — 46
- Isabel Caterer — 47
- Victoria Atkinson — 48
- Emma Kitching — 48
- Daniel O'Connor — 49
- George Denison — 50

St Peter's RC High School, Gloucester
- Hayley Beamish — 50
- David Ryan — 51
- Emily Lucas — 52
- Armani Saintil — 52
- Annie Copley — 53
- Chris Jones — 54
- Joan Ashcroft — 54
- Jack Breeze — 55
- April Jenner — 56
- Elizabeth Davies — 56
- Shannon Haigh — 57
- Lauren Bundy — 58
- Lindsey Browning — 58
- Tom Hanley — 59
- Beccy Collinson — 60
- Hannah Ahern — 60
- Charlotte Withers — 61
- Jessica Jones — 62
- Rebecca Shiers — 62
- Michael Smith — 63
- Tom Wilkinson — 63
- Charlotte Fox — 64
- Alex Jones — 64
- Gemma Hendzel — 65
- Melissa Davis — 66

Samantha Robertson	66
Amy Parkin	67
Reanne Umali	67
James Noble	68
Edel Quinn	68
Hayley Dalley	69
Laurence Wilcock	70
Dominic Gray	70
Daniel Sullivan	71
Clare Aldred	71
Portia Costanza-Brown	72
Steffi Saleem Sardar	72
Gregory Henry	73
Lauradana Day	74
Lawrence Jenkin	74
Lucy Church	75
John Lloyd Gardiner	76
Aleksander Konarski	76
Abigail Whitelow	77
Harriet Walsh	78
Ross Ellis	78
Yazmine Jackson	79
Dawn Collins	80
Martin Micallef	80
Esme Gibbons	81
David Hearfield	82
Grace McAvoy	82
Stephen Parsons	83
William Craig	84
Lucy Reeves	84
Lucinda Behan	85
Sean McLoughlin	86
Rebecca Holgate	86
Aimie Moore	87
Nico Lanciano	87
Sian Hopson	88
Jessica Moore	88
Ben Kelly	89

Jade Turner	90
Michael Braicu	90
Beth-Ann Davies	91
Matt Davies	92
Harriet Anne Layhe	92
Sacha Fullerton	93
Kerry Dooner	94
Chad Kiely	94
Harry Lawlor	95
Damien John Walker	95
Emily Nash	96
Abby Collins	96
Shareena Toth	97
Danielle Weir	98
Robyn Fowler	99
Nuala Darke	99

Thomas Keble School

Lianne Stimpson	100
Clair Gittings	100
Louise Durman	101
Katie Ponting	101
Rachel Conboy	102
Ruth Fitzgerald	102
James Thorburn	103
Hannah Baker	104
Lauren Bain	104
Rob Rogers	105
Christopher Job	106
Lisa Rice	106
Daniel Rotter	107
Dave Brook	108
Daniel Browning	108
Edward Parsloe	109
Josie Fowler	110
Tom Prosser	110
Brighid Nathanson	111
Stella Watts	111

Camilla Allan	112
Felicity Venning	113
Miranda Love	114
Jonathan Weaver	114
Heather Wood	115
Daniel Weston	115
Emma McCartney	116
Tom Jones	116
Theo Durrant	117
Ross Collins	118
Joshua Hale	118
Leah Cratchley	119
Jonathan Brown	119
Katherine Warner	120
Georgina Bullough	121
Becky Short	122
Rhiain Nathanson	122
Matthew Dean	123
Emma Townsend	123
Luke Nash	124
Simon Brown	124
Shane Rowles	125
Mitchell Tudor	125
Sarah Finch	126
Philip Buckle	126
Dan Flack	127
Lindsey Bentall	128
Katy Costigan	128
Kirsten Webb	129
Holly King	130
Kelly Clark	131
Saskia Stainer-Hutchins	132
Sam Underwood	132
Ashley Birkin	133
Stephanie Nash	133
Eleanor Seager	134
Craig Stephens	134
Sara Sharp	135

Ann-Marie Hands	135
Stuart Austin	136
Laurie Merchant	136
Kerry Brown	137
Chris Lees	137
Richard Montague	138
Jamie Goode	138
Clair Akhurst	139
Michael Ryan	139
Alex Dennis	140
Rebecca Cook	140
Kerrie Shaylor	141
Samantha Jones	142
Rachel Rendell	142
Ysobel Baker	143
Gabriel Raeburn	144
Jenna Chudley	144
Ben Scrivens	145
Arthur Milroy	146
Emily Mayo	146
Amy Finch	147
Laurence King	147
Samantha Barclay	148
Matt Saunders	148
Kate Gaskell	149
Dean Turner	149
Sophie Whitfield	150
Saffa McGlynn	151
Robbie Gillett	152
Andrew Roberts	152
Matt Hobbs	153
Peter Dempsey	153
Simon Whiting	154
Becky Hathaway	154
Kate Carpenter	155
Richard Hendy	155
Alex Hill	156
Naomi Nobes	156

James Hemming	157
Kate Espley	158
Craig Banyard	158
Becki Short	159
Alice Crick	160
Laura Northcott	160
Paul Stephens	161
James Westerby	162
Jamie Ponting	162
Grant Tudor	163
Sadie Whiting	164
Rebecca Starkiss	164
Michael Eedle	165
Ben Payne	166
Jenny Warner	167
Holly Brown	168
Matthew Flagg	168
Emily Coles	169

The Poems

SCULPTURES

S unshine was glittering in the autumn morning
C asting shadows
U nder the trees
L eaves start to change colour
P eople amazed by the shades
T hey looked at the beautiful train track
U p in the trees the birds are singing happily
R eally amazing chair sculpture
E ach oak tree is sparkled with gold, chestnut colours
S uch beautiful autumn colours.

Katie Johnson (12)
Belmont School (Area Special)

SUNSHINE

S unlight peeping out
U nder the trees
N ow it is autumn
S o lovely and bright
H unt for sculptures
I n the forest
N oisy children having fun
E verywhere.

Hannah Lewis (14)
Belmont School (Area Special)

Autumn

A mazing
U nbelievable
T elltale signs
U nbelievable
M agical
N ow autumn is here.

Richard White (13)
Belmont School (Area Special)

Autumn

A utumn has come, the leaves are
U p in the trees
T he colours are changing
U nder the autumn sun
M oving leaves in the gentle breeze
N ature is all around.

Charlotte Berry (12)
Belmont School (Area Special)

Autumn Leaves

L ots of leaves
E vergreen
A pple trees
V ery colourful
E vergreen
S ilently falling.

Tanya Wise (13)
Belmont School (Area Special)

SUNSHINE

S hining through the trees
U nder the trees we walk
N ext we pick up leaves
S hiny purple beetles crawling
H ere we hear some birds whistling
I n the trees autumn leaves make lovely colours
N ow we are on our way back
E nd of our sunny day.

Jamie Wright (13)
Belmont School (Area Special)

FOREST

F ull of trees
O verhanging leaves
R eally beautiful colours
E vergreen
S unlight peeping through
T ranquillity.

Daniel Kear (14)
Belmont School (Area Special)

TREES

T he trees are beautiful trees
R eady to see a beautiful oak tree?
E veryone look at a beautiful sculpture
E ach boy looks at a beautiful leaf
S ome boys look at beautiful trees.

Binyaameen Watson (12)
Belmont School (Area Special)

MUD

Mud in my fingernails
Mud between my toes
Mud in your earholes
Grass up your nose!
Mould in our pyjamas
Fleas in your bed
Maggots in your slippers
Flies on your head.

Aimee Kirby-Giles (15)
Belmont School (Area Special)

GO-KART RACING

It flies round the track
Making no sound at all.
The wheels go so fast
Spinning round like a ball.
The engine is big and bulky
For a high speed race.
All the other drivers
Can't keep up the pace.
The wheels make skids
As I go round the bend
And I lose control
Just before the end.

Lee Powell (12)
Maidenhill School

MY TV

I enter my room
And there it is,
My twenty-eight inch box,
It's really the biz.

I switch it on
The volume is loud,
The picture is great,
It makes me proud.

It might be a drama
Or maybe a cartoon,
I'll settle in front
And find out soon.

Chocolate to my left,
Cola to my right,
Laughing my head off,
In for a good night.

The hours go by
I hear the word 'bed'
I don't think so Mum,
The villain ain't dead.

I go to school
Yes I realise that,
But it's not a good reason
To move from where I'm sat.

I have to give in,
Mum's bigger than me,
Don't worry my darling box,
I'll see you for GMTV.

Jake Martin (12)
Maidenhill School

THROUGHOUT THE YEARS

Throughout the years I've waited for you
For the magical things and the thing that you do
For my love I will wait for this day I dream
And the first day we sat and drank from the stream
And the beauty of its waterfalls in the lake
All these memories

Throughout the years
I shed those tears
From the wonderful days
But now it's all in a haze
It's locked in a dream
As weird as it may seem
Until we meet in the skies
Up there

Throughout the magical years I know
From the spring, summer and winter's snow
We were one and free
We were meant to be
Through wonderful years

Until the day
You were sent away
When we drank from the spring water
And had our first daughter
The wonderful days

The joys in life were great for you
The joys in life are powerful too
From the earth I stand on
With our daughter and son
We miss you and these wonderful dreams
Even though death as it seems
Took you away
From those wonderful days

We pray for you
We miss you too
We wish you were here
As we cry our tears
We know you are watching so we all keep smiling
And remember the day
Throughout the years.

Sophie Prosser (14)
Maidenhill School

THE PATTERNED TORTOISE!

In the garden near a rock
Rests the old tortoise,
Eating the lettuce and tomato without a care.

Eating like a boy with sweets,
Its shell is armour against a fox.
The shell is so beautiful and strong
No beast could destroy the ultimate armour.

As slow as a snail,
But as strong as metal casing.
This interesting reptile moves like clockwork,
Tick-tock with no care at all.

The legs and head enter
The cage that acts as protection
From the ever-attacking nature.

Fearsome foxes and wicked wolves
Can't hurt this cold-blooded
Tortoise.

Christopher Budding (12)
Maidenhill School

MY SISTER

My poem is about my sister,
If she ran away I wouldn't miss her!
All she does is scream and shout,
It makes me want to knock her out!
She's in love with a band called Busted,
I think that they're old and crusted!
She supports a team called Chelsea
Will they win the league? We'll see.
She is such a huge tomboy,
She likes to play with her Action Man toy.

Hannah Chivers (12)
Maidenhill School

MY EXPLODING POEM

S hocking explosions that make a big *bang!*
C rackling equipment that is always breaking
I nvisible problems floating by
E xploding experiments always going wrong
N ever knowing what might happen
C lasses scream as the chemicals explode
E xperiments are always so much fun!

Stacey Slocombe (12)
Maidenhill School

LIFE

Life is full of twists and turns,
Life is like a book,
Each page represents a new day,
Life, in life we can explore and create new things.
One minute someone can be on top of the world,

The next someone can't see the point in
Living because they are so depressed.
Life can be a very strange thing at times
But as the old saying goes, 'That's life'.

Toby Hinde (11)
Maidenhill School

THE GHOST UNDER THE FLOOR

As you see it,
You'll never guess
Through the front door I go.

Bang! Something slammed the door.
The ancient-looking stairs creak,
I walked towards the fire.

Aarrghh! - It springs to life.
These strange monkey statues . . .
Laugh . . . Aarrghh . . . Get me out of here.

The floorboards creak,
He appears white and pale,
'Give me my brandy!'

He yells!
'Please get me out of here.'
I'll tell you more about

His cutlass that's a sword.
'I'm the Cornish ghost, get out!'
I'm going, I run to the door.

Hurrah! It opens,
I do not stop
I remember that blood-red carpet.

Daniel McIntosh (12)
Maidenhill School

SEASONS OF THE SUN!

Spring, summer, autumn, winter
Every year's the same
Round and round the seasons go
Like a party game
Spin the leaves from green to brown
Spin them to gold
Chase the clouds across the sky
Paint a yellow sun
Then the rain comes tumbling down
Spoiling all the fun.

Holly Taylor (12)
Maidenhill School

BECAUSE I CARE

There are
so many things I want to be for
you and so many things I want to do.
Play games, comfort you and look after you
day and night, but the most important
thing of all is to be
your friend for the
rest of my
life.

Aaran Leach (12)
Maidenhill School

PEOPLE DON'T KNOW

People don't know what it feels like,
To long for some love like I do,
Yet when you find someone special,
You know that they can't love you.

People don't know what it feels like,
To have heartache every day,
You meet that special person,
Then they go away.

People don't know what it feels like,
To hurt in so many ways,
Why do I put myself through this
And scan through the desperate days?

People don't know what it feels like,
To choke on sorrowful tears,
All I need is some love
To see me through my years.

People don't know what it feels like
To have pain eat away at your soul
And leave you with nothing but sadness
With no love to fill that hole.

People don't know what it feels like,
To cry yourself to sleep
And have dreams of love and kindness
Haunt you whilst you sleep!

Beth Sutton (14)
Newent Community School

FLIGHT

Taking off in a big balloon
There's so much to see!
We start up north and work our way down to the south.

Scottish Borders, looking over the foggy hills
One glimpse of the scary creature
Would be one of the funniest things to see

I fly across the big blue sky
I see the birds that fly so high
I wish I was one of them too
But in a way I am
In this big balloon

Coming down from good old Scotland
Passing over the Yorkshire Dales
Looking over
And seeing all the hundreds of miniature people

Now I look at the huge clouds
The beautiful angels sit on top
When does all this fun stop?

Hannorah Stephens (12)
Newent Community School

BEST FRIENDS

Back in September when I started my new school
I was really quite nervous but hoped it would be cool.

I met loads of new friends and we got on really well
But no one is as good as you because you're my best pal.

Can you remember the times when we were really small?
We used to sit on the play mat and dribble and drool.

We've done everything together, even learning to swim,
We are so close, it's like you're my twin.

As we grow older new friends we will make
But I'm not worried as you'll always be my mate.

Lauren Hobbs (11)
Newent Community School

NEVER FORGET

When it first hit
The very first one
Then it hit the second one
Down they fell
One by one
And out jumped people
Before those looking on
The emergency services tried to help
But many died
One by one
Some innocents tried to help
But all they could do
Was to look blindly on
As the shock went through the world
That many had died
Helping another one
You can't look back
Yet it's hard to look on
For those who lost
A beloved one
Never forget that
Catastrophic day
As the towers crashed down
One by one.

Siobhan Vye (12)
Newent Community School

BOYS AND GIRLS

Boys think they're cool
Girls prefer school
Boys play with snares
Girls do their hair

Models, bikes and cars
Make-up, shopping and chocolate bars
Girls and hair gels
Boys and nice smells

Baggy jeans
Fashion queens
Off their heads
Like their beds

Like plenty of dirt
Moan if they get hurt
Fighting for kicks
Sexy chicks.

Stephanie Mowbray (13)
Newent Community School

DOLPHINS WHO SWIM IN THE SEA

The dolphins swim in the peaceful sea,
Under a sky of cumulonimbus clouds,
They dart and play under the azure waters,
They have no responsibilities and none are given.

Beneath the rippled surface they dance,
Skimming the earthen bottom they smile
And leaping into the air they laugh,
They do this day after day, mile after mile.

Meanwhile I sit at home or at school,
Responsibilities pile high up to the sky
I dream and yearn to do what I choose,
Like the dolphins who swim in the sea.

Lucy Ryan (12)
Newent Community School

WINTER DAY

Now here comes the winter nights,
Dark and frosty sights,
The moon glistens on the ice,
Like it's dancing and prancing like little mice,

The trees all lose their leaves,
And too, it brings a bitter breeze,
The heat is removed and cold replaced,
We all feel a bit displaced.

Christmas is nearly here,
The children's thoughts are all nice and clear,
They have finished deciding what they want,
They send their letters off to Sant.

The icicles are hanging off,
Now's the time we catch a cough,
The frost is shimmering to the sky,
Like fairies flying up high.

We all can't wait till Christmas Day,
The decorations are already up and we're away,
The air is colder than before
And now, the snow's plunging in with the more.

Vicky Howell (13)
Newent Community School

FIFTY METRES

Up on the blocks, with my head in the clouds.
Bending down to touch my toes.
Hearing the gun go off.
Diving in.
Kicking my legs as hard as I can.
Reaching forward, pulling back.
Curving my hand each time.
At the end and turning round,
Going under, push off and
Kicking with all my might.
Winning, I'm winning, the end's in sight.
I feel for the wall, I've got it, I've *won!*

Kate Richards (11)
Newent Community School

THE WAVES

As the lamp raised higher in the sky,
Its colour changed from a deep golden red
To a bright yellowy orange.
Slowly the tide calmed and birds appeared.
Body-shaped shadows grew as they reached the sea's edge.
Boats waited, surrounded with old rope and nets,
As they fled like they were escaping
Into the depths.
Later they reappeared like a trail of ants,
Getting bigger as they got closer.
Everyone scrambling, searching through their nets,
To see what they'd caught.
Grabbing fish and shells one by one,
Throwing them into buckets.
So they hurried to finish before dusk.

Gemma Louise Meyer (14)
Rednock School

THE DAZING CORNER

I was crouched in the corner,
Of a heaving pub.
All I could see was bright lights,
As I squinted in the mad bustle of people.

I was insignificant to everyone,
As people brushed past.
Some gave me a brief view
And then gave a sharp 'tut'.

I took a deep gulp
And felt my lungs soothe in alcohol.
I thought my troubles were over,
Only then I felt this pain.

I felt a strong stinging sensation
And felt my lips crinkle in pain.
Crumbs of salt clung to my lips,
Making me cringe in agony.

Then all of a sudden
I came to terms with myself.
I realised I was not welcome,
I was to go.

I stepped outside and looked around,
Yet wherever I looked I knew I wasn't welcome.
I quickly went to get some food,
Fish and chips, then I would go.

James Shelley (13)
Rednock School

Danny's New Girlfriend

Danny always had new girlfriends
They dump him then they mock
But now there's someone different
A new girl on the block

This new girl was called Lucy
She's extremely pretty and slim
Let's hope Danny can hold on to her
She isn't your average Kim

Up 'til now Danny's mum was worried
He couldn't be a seedy bachelor type
But now she had met sweet Lucy
There seemed no need to gripe

It all seemed a bit surreal
She might become his wife
Then Danny strolled in and said,
'Mum, Dad, please meet the woman who has changed my life.'

A year late and I realised
This was not just another silly fling
There was now a ring on her finger
They were getting wed in spring!

Lois Tucker (13)
Rednock School

Battle For The Shore

The waves start as a ripple swarming to the shore,
like an invading army.
Then they rise into a hill of moving water as they advance.
Then shrink as they reach the land as if cowering from an attack.
Then the wave runs out of water and breaks into the sand barracks.

Then spawns as a rush of water running up the shingle,
Into battle with the shore.
For a second it stops at its peak,
Then retreats back to the sea and disappears into a wall of water.

Joseph Dimery (13)
Rednock School

DANNY'S NEW GIRLFRIEND

I saw her walking past me,
I thought I recognised her,
As she turned round the corner
I knew who it must be.

She asked me to meet her,
Of course I said yes,
She came to confess
How much she loved me.

The next day,
My friends told me
She wasn't right for me.
As I walked round the corner,
I knew I wouldn't like what I was about to see.
Her, my dream girl, kissing a boy,
That was the end of us.

I'd had my share of girlfriends,
I gave up on them a while ago,
Now, instead, I am living my dream,
I play for Liverpool football team.

Natalie Williams (14)
Rednock School

WAVES

The sea was slightly creased as if a cloth has wrinkles on it,
The sea blazed gold as the sun slowly faded,
Like a woman lowering her lamp lower and lower.
The sky, a pink and purple haze, fluffy white balls soaking
in the colour.
The lamp lowered itself further,
Black puddles forming on the glass green water.
The waves sighed like a sleeper whose breath comes and goes,
Bubbles emerged from the white foam as the wave surged itself
up the sand bank and then retired.
Only a faint line stood between a black sea of wrinkles
and a smoky pink sky.
The lamp lowered itself further,
So that the soft wrinkles were almost rubbed out.
The lamp lowered itself for the last time,
And then an immense blanket of black swept up everything,
Nothing was able to avoid this darkness that hugged the world.
Everything was motionless.
The sea was indistinguishable from the sky,
Except that the sea was slightly creased as if it had wrinkles in it.

Sophie Scott (14)
Rednock School

THE WATERS OF LOVE

The water of love floods all,
There is nothing I see which isn't love itself,
I dissolve into water at the wave of his hand
And flow away like a flood.

It flows over the devastated Earth,
I drink, unsatisfied,
The liquid waterfalls consume all I see,
They turn into love.

The sound of praise defeats all doubters,
T he pain of the world cannot defeat our love,
The sound of gratitude floods all others,
The tide of love rises again.

It bursts through all boundaries,
I feel safe and warm,
The passion explodes shamed eardrums,
Nothing can influence these tides of love.

Lizzie Burgin (14)
Rednock School

DANNY'S NEW GIRLFRIEND
(A brother in love)

There stood Lucy, slender and tall,
Dressed in red in my front hall,
Child-like she seemed to me but not to my brother,
Who described her as a woman and claimed he did love her,
My mother looked please, happy not at all mad,
She thought of those Peggies and Debs who had made him so sad,
He was always getting dumped by girls who would hang from his arm,
Though this Lucy lass, could she do any harm?
Darling Lucy, the young woman in red,
'She's beautiful Dan,' these were the only words I said.
I looked into her eyes, she smiled with delicate teeth,
I'm sure my brother wouldn't feel that much grief.
I asked her to meet me out back in an hour,
Sixty minutes later I met her, oh how she did glower,
'I love Danny, Ian, don't be a clown.'
I walked away with an embarrassed frown.
Darling Lucy, the young woman in red,
'She's beautiful Dan,' these were the only words I said.

Jenny Caesar (13)
Rednock School

Listening

    Listen to the waves
    Listen to the waves
Everything has its own pattern.
The pebbles move with the rhythm of the waves,
Making a rolling sound as they go.
The waves sigh like a sleeper whose breath comes
and goes unconsciously.
They sweep a thin veil of white water across the sand,
like a bride's dress.
Suddenly it breathes back in, pulling the sand away jealously.
The waves lap in a dreamy seduction against the horizon.
The sea yawns a long mournful yawn,
This signals the dawn of life,
Fish swim, dolphins dance.
The sun rises
Then it sinks back down like a feather floating gently,
As if in reverse everything calms,
Soon, once again, the sea will wake.
    Listen to the waves.
    Listen to the waves.

Rose Chard (13)
Rednock School

The Waves

The sun had not yet risen,
The sea and sky were as one,
Gradually the sky grew lighter,
To greet the morning sun.

The tide brought with it a veil
Of white water along the sand,
The waves drew back and forth,
Revealing a pale, golden land.

The colours of the sunbathed land,
Were flickering and bright,
On the horizon, like a woman's arm,
Was holding a flaming light.

The sea was becoming transparent,
It lay sparkling and bathed in gold,
Gentle ripples spread across the water,
As the golden waves calmly rolled.

Fergus Harris (13)
Rednock School

APOCALYPSE

And the hellish fires of Heaven burns,
As the sun fades and moon does turns,
Why, oh why, couldn't we learn
From what they tried to teach us?

If we could have only known,
Then just maybe could have grown,
A garden, a field, sweet harvest to be sown,
Instead of this darkling menace.

Now, because not, the apocalypse has come
And the world is surely done,
Oh well, we've had our bit of fun
And now our lives are over.

And the hellish fires of Heaven burn,
As the sun fades and the moon does turn,
Why, oh why, didn't we learn?
Now there are none to teach us.

Jenny Hoskins (13)
Rednock School

The Cross Sea

The sun had not yet risen,
As I started to come back in,
The sheet above me burst out colours
Of pink, white and blue,
It was so peaceful.

The sun was on its way up,
As I was calmly lying on the golden sand,
Until I felt a sharp pain of something kicking and jumping in me
And I knew it was happening again.

The sun was blazing down and making me sparkle,
Big things were swimming in me,
Making me look like a wrinkled cloth,
It was so loud and noisy,
I couldn't hear myself.

The sun was on its way down
When I decided to go out again,
Away from all this madness,
Can't they pick on someone their own size?
Do they think how jumping around in me hurts?

The sun had not yet risen,
As I was calmly lying on the golden sand,
I knew I would have to go through all that
Madness and pain again.
I'll get my own back one day, don't worry.

Stephanie May (13)
Rednock School

THE SHADOWY CORNER

I sat in the shadowy corner,
My lips stinging with salt.
As the cold beer ran down my throat,
My insides started to melt.

I didn't know where I was,
I must have walked miles that evening.
I sat, tired and hungry in a sleazy pub,
With salt all over my uniform.

Street lamps winked outside,
Reflected in my beer.
My stomach rumbled and I cried,
For I had missed home all year.

I wasn't very happy, but counted myself lucky.
I sat quietly. I listened.
Voices didn't stammer,
My eyes were freed from the ache of khaki.

Exhausted though I was,
I was also hungry.
My mind flashed back to the café,
For I was having second thoughts.

A slight breeze blew along the dark, deserted streets,
Rustling leaves on trees and washing on balconies.
I took another swig of beer,
As I sat in the shadowy corner.

Benjamin Vick (14)
Rednock School

SENSES OF THE SEA

I watched. The golden sun had not yet risen,
The sea was attached to the sky with the devotion of a mother and child.
The wrinkled sheet of sea slowly crept towards the shore,
Then rose, heaped itself and slid back with a sigh,
Like a sleeper whose breath comes and goes unconsciously.

I listened. The sound of a distant crash of waves on the rocks,
The lonely cry of a seagull.
I felt. The shingle fell through my fingers like rain dripping from drooping branches.
The water flowed like velvet over my feet.

I tasted the fresh sea air which filled my lungs with gold.
I licked my lips and tasted the salty residue left as a gift from the sea.

I watched once more, the sun rose out of the sea like a ball of fire
And all around the sea blazed gold.

Fiona Speak (13)
Rednock School

WATER OF LOVE

The flame is still burning,
With the love that grows between us.
My lonesome heart keeps on yearning,
When I see all angles of love.

I hear a silent whisper,
Just as the gentle flow of water meets the valley.
The beautiful flowers become higher,
When I see all angles of love.

The soft sprinkles of the fountain touch the sun
And a blaze of light shines down onto the golden sand.
Inspired by the only one,
When I see all angles of love.

Finally darkness draws near
And the candle begins to flicker.
The memory of my precious tear,
No longer sees angles of love.

Carly Hillier (14)
Rednock School

DANNY'S NEW GIRLFRIEND!

Danny fell in love that spring,
I thought it was just a silly fling.
He'd had so many girlfriends before,
They were less, but this was more.

Was Lucy another to add to his collection?
Was it me or did he have some more affection?
She looked so fragile,
As if she were to run a mile.

But when I saw Danny glowing,
I just felt a sense of knowing.
She was so pretty,
To add to this she was also witty.

Danny fell in love that spring,
I can already hear the church bells ring!

Verity Everett (14)
Rednock School

MY TIDALS OF LOVE

When these four words are mentioned
It makes me think of so many things.
It makes me think that there is no angle
No angle the world can assume
Nothing that the love in my eyes cannot make
    Into a symbol of love.

When these four words are spoken
I think that love must be calm like the sea.
Special, soothing, safe and secure.
Everything flows over the Mississippi
    Over a devastated Earth.

When these four words are whispered
It makes me think of you
The person who this is all about
You and the precise geometry of your hand
And when I gaze at it,
    It dissolves me into water.

When these four words are muttered
I flow away in a flood of love
Which raises a sound of praise
Not all the poisonous tides of the blood
I have spilt can influence my tidals of love.

Danielle Smith (13)
Rednock School

SYMBOLS OF LOVE

The calling seagulls flying high remind me of that night you made me cry in pain,
The youthful colours of the beach remind me of that marriage speech and hope,
The waves gently lapping over the sands remind me of his soothing hands that used to touch my soul,

The stones pressed cold upon my feet remind me of where
we used to meet,
I didn't feel the cold then,
But the beach still makes me feel that some day
You will reveal
Why you walked away.

Chloe Williams (13)
Rednock School

THE WAVES

The sun had not yet risen,
The sea blended with the sky,
Apart from clouds that drifted,
For they shall never die.

As the waves neared the shore
And broke across the sand,
They reached out ever further,
Just like a slender hand.

Jagged rocks are taken,
Rounded and smoothed,
Soft pebbles cluster on the sand,
My pain within is soothed.

As the sun ascended,
The brightness lit the skies,
Resembling a bonfire,
That burnt within my eyes.

As I looked across the sea,
A magnificent sight I saw,
The sea blazed a fiery gold,
The waves lapping forever more.

Richard Walton (13)
Rednock School

A Night Away From The Battlefield

The dingy corner of the bar,
Cradles the soldier, drinking beer,
For this very drink, he's travelled far,
The amber lights concealed his fear.

He's marched miles today, gradually tiring,
Through winding streets and pebbled roads,
The warm night air has stopped him sighing,
His back is screaming, from pains of loads.

He walks through towns, where washing hangs
And drifts of steak bring memories of home,
His skin is sliced, his head, it bangs,
A café stands there all alone.

He opens the door, the smell, it reeks,
Of damp and dirt on dish and plate,
He goes on in, company he seeks,
But his clothes are met with looks of hate.

He sits down anyway, hunger pangs grow,
With an aroma of chips his eyes shine bright,
But then a whistle - surely, no,
All are silent as the night.

The bombshell soars onto the floor,
The small café breaks into flame,
He opens his eyes, death at his door
And on his lips, a whispered name.

Dora Meredith (13)
Rednock School

THAT GIRL

If I were with you for one moment I would feel immortal,
Yet my knees would collapse beneath me.
Oh how I wish you were mine,
We would go out, dance and dine.

We would be like pen and paper,
Destined to be together.
This love is right, this love is to savour,
Let's be together for eternity,
Meet at the canteen, just you and me.

She walks past me swishing her hair,
It's so cruel she doesn't know I'm here.
She's so popular, talented and keen,
How can I win her when she doesn't even know me?

I am a spot freak, a total geek,
No looks, no style,
Just sad old me.
If only we had the chance for our love to blossom,
It wouldn't matter what we wear, just as long as we're together.

I know I have to come out of my dreamworld,
As this love can never be.
It will never come to pass,
As she has chosen him not me.

Sara Price (13)
Rednock School

SOLDIER

I watch the amber lights winking in my beer,
Sitting in a shadowy corner,
Of a pub in a sleazy district,
Near Edinburgh,
I had walked miles that night,
Not knowing what to look for.
I didn't know!

The smell of steak reminds one of home,
That little house where I once lived,
Long, long ago!
My stomach, it rumbles hard,
I have not eaten for days,
Just peanuts - the salt stinging,
Dried, cracked skin from an asthma attack.

It was worth going to the pub that night,
Just to sit quietly,
To listen to voices,
To have my eyes free from the ache of khaki.

A long way down the street
Was a lonely cafe,
The door opened,
The breath of hot,
Damp and dirty air,
Decided me against it,
I was too hungry to care.

The windows dripped with condensation,
The damp air filled my uniform,
A short silence fell, conspicuous and unwelcome,
I needed something to eat,
Fish and chips filled me up fine - then I would go.

Marcus Tibbitts (13)
Rednock School

SYMBOLS OF MY LOVE

There is no angle the world can assume,
Which the love in my eye
Cannot make into a symbol of love.

The sea, powerful,
Doing anything to reach its goal,
Destroying, eroding,
The rock of disbelievers.

The sun,
A source of energy,
That will never run out,
Always there for someone.

The sky,
Blocked out by clouds,
But always there,
Like my love for you.

A jigsaw linking together,
The interlocking
Of our twin souls
To see the full picture.

A bomb,
When it hits there is an explosion
Of emotion and passion,
No one can escape it.

As time goes by,
All these emotions come together as one,
The sea, the sun, the sky
A jigsaw and a bomb.
As symbols of my love.

Jennifer Pedrick (13)
Rednock School

THE GIRLFRIENDS

Standing there she looked about,
Whilst the Bestoes checked her out.
'She looks alright,' Ian said,
But Mother answered, 'What a ghastly red!'

Danny stood there utterly stunned,
He looked at Lucy, who gently hummed.
'How can they even criticise
The girl I love so deep inside?'

Eventually the huddle broke
And Mum and Dad in turn spoke;
'Danny we know it has been some time,
Since you've met a girl, oh so fine.'

'We want the best for you and her
And we can see that you love each other,
So we've decided we will not pry
Until you find a place to buy!'

So now the Bestoes have had their wish
For their son to seek someone to fit the dish!
Just one more wish, a hope, was needed
Which was soon to be happily succeeded.

One year on from that fine spring
And Ian came home with a girl he did bring
She stood there calmly, on Ian's arm
And spoke out slowly, completely calm,
'Mum, Dad, Danny and Lucy,
This is the girl who has changed my life!'

Kim Blick (13)
Rednock School

THE WAVES

The sun had not yet risen,
The sea lapped up onto the fine white sand,
There was no sound,
The wave paused and then drew out again.

The sea was not like that at night,
It was like a ravenous monster,
Eating the old wine bottle left by the tide,
The wave paused and then drew out again.

The monster roared loudly at the rocks,
Eating away at them over time,
Foaming at the mouth, crashing into them,
The wave paused and then drew out again.

When you look at the horizon,
Dividing the sea from the sky,
Turning crimson, amber and golden,
As the sun rises from below the ravenous monster.

Becky Allen (13)
Rednock School

AFRICA

Feeling good as I think of my holiday in Africa,
Amber skies with the silhouette of the Savannah,
I gaze at the elegant dance of the gazelle.
Zip! Zap! chatter the cheetahs fighting for their dinner.
A herd of elephants storm towards the drinking hole.
Holding their heads up high, the giraffes are
The skyscrapers of the animal world.

Faiza Hadi (11)
Ribston Hall High School

WAR AND PEACE

Gone, the broken, grey, blackened buildings burnt by bombs,
Gone, the fear that falls from the sky.
We are here with clear blue skies,
Where green and brown crown the end of the summer.

In the morning the heavy dew clings for life onto
Silver webs, the work of the spider.
The crimsons, oranges, browns and yellows wake
To greet the fading greens of summer.

Where the flower once stood so proud,
Bright against the emerald,
The dull seed head now waits to spill its treasures,
To renew next summer's bounty.

The air echoes with life.
Robins sing to the reapers with songs of joyful notes.
Keeping rhythm,
A great spotted woodpecker taps his hollow tune.

Movement in the sky waves goodbye
To the swallow, as he plans his journey south.
With the coming of the autumn, birds
Fly from berries to corn, making the most of this short feast.

Fields are alive with animals looking for an opportunity.
Long-tailed mice and harvest mice
Jump in and out of boys harvesting the corn.
With patience, the red fox waits.

A sundew plant shows a tiny white flower,
Small beside the deadly nightshade.
With leaves like hands, its berries
Sit as tempting sweets on plates of green.

And back home, the land of smoke and brick.
Are they safe?
Are they well?
Are they happy?

Natasha Frewer (12)
Ribston Hall High School

MUM

Twelve years have gone by,
But Mum's love to me never dies,
She's still as jolly as can be,
And always forgives troublesome me,
Arguments that have occurred,
Have always magically disappeared.

The humour Mum creates
Is funny and always great,
She knows what we like,
From music to clothes and even our choice of bike,
Help we need is always there,
Which is always brought with love and care.

Love is always there,
With our mum who is filled with care,
She's not for sale, she's one of a kind,
Love and friendship is what you'll find
With a mum like ours, she's the best,
She is and always will be better than the rest!

Elizabeth Sheils (12)
Ribston Hall High School

THE PATH OF GOLD

Leaves crunch under your feet,
The colours blend into each other.
The wind echoes through your head,
And swirls around you.
Causing you to stumble,
Onto the crunchy golden bed.
Lying on the path,
The trees look tall,
But they are a comfort,
They are the golden walls around you.
But they cannot protect you,
From the cold, icy wind . . .

Nadia Tavana (12)
Ribston Hall High School

SANTA CLAUS

Everyone was calm on Christmas Day
Until Santa came upon his sleigh,
He was dressed in red from head to toe
And his beard was as white as snow.
He had a chubby face with big blue eyes
And he went downstairs for his Christmas pies.
He filled the stockings, one by one,
One for the daughter and one for the son.
Then when he had made everyone's day,
Santa Claus then flew away.

Danielle Talbot (11)
Ribston Hall High School

THE END... IS NEAR...

The misty air, so creepy and thick,
The hard cold ground frosted and sharp,
The light ahead, so dim, so faint,
Then the voices whisper through the dying trees,
The end... is near...

No other sound is heard,
No animals cower in the remains of a bush,
No birds sing in perfect harmony,
All is silent,
Apart from the whisper,
The end... is near...

Laura Holdsworth (12)
Ribston Hall High School

SUMMER

De blazing sun is so much fun,
De blossom swirls away,
De orange, de red, de spring is dead,
De summer sun should stay.

De blue in de sea is just for me,
De sun is way up high,
De dolphins play, day should stay,
De day could float on by.

De children scream with a happy beam,
De ice creams are given out,
De swimming pool is very cool,
De children all shout.

Heather Owen (12)
Ribston Hall High School

PURE THOUGHTS OF BEAUTY

My fantasies are my creative inspiration.
A diamond-glazed finish is engraved in my heart.
A distant memory of snow, broken,
Disjointed time. I am devoted to you,
Sweet Bliss.
A sparkle in the moonlight from
Tears of an angel's wings.

The blonde-kissed fate,
The freckles in my heart
Causing my heart to bleed, bleeding
The sour red of a rose's pressed petals.
That, which you gave
Once you cared, back then.

The heart's cry of pain, of love unspoken.
Mine no longer of pain in which was felt, hope.
No longer to try or to weep, if only you
Call out to my name.
I whisper. The gentle nightingale sings
Songs of love bringing a star
Shining in the moonlight.
I am left.
A silent ocean in your eyes of everlasting
Pain was caught by the mist,
Amongst us we felt, crystal,
A shield of love.

Natalie Hall (17)
Ribston Hall High School

DANIEL

Nine long months
And there he was.
A cute little baby
Whatever he does.
His fingers so small,
The way he crawls.
He is my brother, Daniel!

I love his chubby, cheeky smile
I forget my worries for a while.
He is funny, huggable and definitely kissable
And his cheeky giggle is completely unmissable.
His eyes are blue, his hair is fair
He is as cuddly as a teddy bear.
He is my brother, Daniel!

Teletubbies is his favourite show,
He really loves Laa-Laa and quite likes Po.
He's like an alarm clock, our little 'tot'
When he shouts really loudly from inside his cot.
There's no such thing as peace and quiet
As living with Daniel is an absolute riot!
I love my brother, Daniel!

Jodie Luce (12)
Ribston Hall High School

WHERE HAVE THEY GONE?

Where have the butterflies gone?
As I look outside I see hurt,
I see disaster.
What used to be peaceful,
Full of life
Is now a truck hurtling down a
Deadly, black frozen river,
Painting the air black with its fumes.
Why can't I see the colour?
Why is this world grey?
Where have the butterflies gone?

Victoria Dovey (11)
Ribston Hall High School

A MORNING'S REFLECTION

To the water-based room limped the sleepy creature,
Jungle of fury gathering above his crown.
From the creature's features,
Spotty mountains erupted
And two black beads looked both up and then down.
Carelessly opening and lazily closing,
A tooth-fringed abyss sucked in a lungful of air.
But closer inspection
Of the ape-like reflection,
Revealed a teenage boy, with gel-filled hair.

Edward Bradley (12)
St Edward's School, Cheltenham

AUTUMN

Like a rainforest canopy,
Glistening golden leaves
Fall softly to the ground,
Rusty reds line the floor
Like a carpet for the Ice Queen.
Brown like tea-stained leaves
Fall to the floor and crunch underfoot.
Bright red and orange
Berries hang like baubles
On a Christmas tree.
A cold sharp breeze
Hangs in the air as if
Trapped in a bubble and
Can't escape.
Robin chatter fills the
Forest with a sense of
Calm and peace.
Hopping around, searching for food,
Braving autumn's charm.
The sun pierces through
And shadows dance
Through the bare, thick
Branches of the translucent trees.
All that remains untouched
In the chilling air are the
Lush greens of the holly
And the warm sense that
Spring will come again.

Becky Taylor (14)
St Edward's School, Cheltenham

MY FATHER

When my father looks in the mirror,
A new man does he see,
A slightly larger version,
Of the one he used to be!

His stomach once so flat and taut,
Has changed its physical form,
No matter how he pounds the street,
It simply won't conform!

His hair once so brown and thick,
Is changing slightly too,
Thin patches are appearing,
In places they shouldn't do!

Grey hairs are also to be seen,
In places rather clearly,
Like silver wings around his ears,
He's been hit by middle-age severely!

My father he has been unwise,
Whilst out in the midday sun,
Has forgotten to wear suncream,
How wrinkled he's become!

Crows' feet have not appeared,
But he has no need to care,
His hobby, ornithology,
Now a resemblance he does bear!

When people see my father,
They say we look alike,
What will my reflection show?
I hope that they're not right!

Laura Tyler (13)
St Edward's School, Cheltenham

THE TIME THE CLOCKS STOPPED

The family anxiously wait by the phone,
Dreading the news they may receive.
They never got to say sorry after the argument,
They never got to give Mummy a hug,
Never got to thank Dad,
For they never returned.

The time the clock stopped,
The time the world stood still,
The time tears were shed,
The time children went to bed
Knowing their mum wouldn't be there to give them a goodnight kiss.
Knowing their dad wouldn't be there to help with their homework.
Knowing how much evil is in the world.

The wife sobs,
The husband weeps,
The sisters cry,
The brothers hold each other,
The parents solemnly hug,
The children are lost.

We all have felt confused,
The question on our tongues is
Why?
The evil speaks for itself,
The innocent had to die.

Emma Jenkins (13)
St Edward's School, Cheltenham

REFLECTIONS ON AUTUMN

How quickly summer's run astray
Wonderful woozy summer days
Weeks that passed in peaceful bliss
Now veiled by dreary autumn's mist.

The pale sun we've known to shine
Is smeared across the grimy sky
Straining through decaying leaves
And hanging strangled in the trees.

The birds that once sang all day long
Have ceased to chatter cheerful song
They have gathered in the skies
And whispered sweet grateful goodbyes.

Dim shadows creep, no longer thin
They bring the bitter winter in
Dance on leaves and tantalise
Lingering clouds from our eyes.

How long the nights, how drab the days
We into dreary bareness gaze
Fog is heavy on our minds
We've left all wakefulness behind.

The days and nights just slither past
The first no different from the last
We just watch the hours go
And wait for the first kiss of snow.

Helen Soutter (14)
St Edward's School, Cheltenham

ME AND MY MIRROR

Oh my, what do I see?
Obviously,
The magnificent me,
My outstandingly gorgeous legs
So fine,
My eyelashes in such a straight line.

Now,
I must keep thin,
Not like a pin,
If I do I'll be in kids' clothes
Too soon,
If that's how it goes.

Oh, mirror, mirror,
Aren't I amazing?
I can't even stop gazing
At my reflection,
Nothing,
Nothing will be interception.

That's how it goes,
Everyone knows
About the best person,
Me,
Duh,
Definitely me,
The truly perfect,
Amazingly gorgeous me.

Isabel Caterer (12)
St Edward's School, Cheltenham

LOOKING AT ME

Oh no, it's a monster,
What shall I do?
I shall have to sprint
On the count of two.

No make-up,
Horrible hair,
Crooked teeth
And a horrible stare.

Horrible figure,
No shape,
She could be a witch,
If she had a cape.

This isn't you,
As you can see,
Looking in the mirror,
It must be me!

Victoria Atkinson (12)
St Edward's School, Cheltenham

HOMELESS

H is for hatred I see in people's eyes.
O is for odyssey, a journey full of lies.
M is for meaningless which my life has now become.
E is for emotions, people assume I have none.
L is for listen to what I have to say.
E is for embarrassment as people turn away.
S is for scum, people mutter every day.
S is for save me! I don't want to be this way.

Emma Kitching (12)
St Edward's School, Cheltenham

REFLECTION

Board arcs up
Board spins
Hand grabs board
Soft landing
Up other side
Board and human
Spin
Land with a bump
Board goes up
Trucks grind
On bar
Wheels spin
Foot pushes
Wheels spin
Faster
Board goes up
Boards slides
On bar
Up the ramp
Good trick
Board flies out
From
Underfeet
Crack!
There goes
His leg
Better luck
Next time.

Daniel O'Connor (12)
St Edward's School, Cheltenham

REFLECTIONS

Reflections appear, then fade away,
As the wind blows across the pond,
Sweeping images off frame,
One minute they're there,
The next they're gone,
Like the freedom of a summer holiday,
Like a chocolate bar,
Like a plant from spring to winter,
Like the humour of a funny joke,
Like a popular craze,
Like a fragrant soap,
Like an ice cream cone,
Like life.
As the water stays still and the wind stops blowing,
The images rest and the picture is set,
Like love,
Like friendship,
Like a monument,
Like a treasured memory,
Like the smile on a photograph,
Like spirit.

George Denison (13)
St Edward's School, Cheltenham

A DOVE

Flying through the air
It silently flaps its wings
Bringing the world peace.

Hayley Beamish (12)
St Peter's RC High School, Gloucester

Conflict

A place which only exists in our world,
on CNN News.
By corrupt and evil powers hurled,
into despairing war.

Where people can't feel safe in bed
at night.
When everyone they knew or loved is dead,
for nothing.

Standing on the roof he sees the flashes
on the horizon.
And down the crumbling, stricken stairs he dashes,
mad with sorrow.

While greedy warlords sit down to feast
in fortified castles,
On their doorstep the people who have least,
starve to death.

When the same warlords could end the suffering and pain,
at a word.
Yet they still choose to sacrifice lives for their own gain,
with all their wealth and power.

What is it that brings these things,
what is the final word?
What causes all the happenings,
that wounds and shakes the world?

Conflict.

David Ryan (12)
St Peter's RC High School, Gloucester

THE AUTUMN HANDOVER

Autumn's face rose up into the sky, dyeing everything he could see, red.
His voice blew all leaves away leaving the trees' hands bare.
The sun sank sadly into the dark mauve horizon,
Leaving winter to take over the land.

The old man's white hair swept over the country,
As snow cried out of the sky's eyes,
Leaving sharp, cold, pointy fingers among the grass.
Winter's soul drifts away in clouds across icy skies.

As a spring breeze drifted back into the air,
The sky's mouth opened to welcome back the sun.
As daffodils danced and swayed,
Dead once again lived, as animals came out from hibernation.
The sky's mouth now screams as summer approaches with a bucket
full of heat.

As summer arrived every corner of Earth was touched by her
elegant hot fingers.
The warmth drifted like the waving of her long golden hair.
Earth was captured in the sparkle of her eye,
But soon enough it was time to say goodbye.

Emily Lucas (13)
St Peter's RC High School, Gloucester

A TIGER

There he is again,
Lying in his den,
Lying in the tall thin grass,
Under the clouds that soon will pass.

As you gaze into the tiger's eye,
A golden deer lazes around,
But the deer collapses to the ground.

Without a sound his pack comes near,
Cos the smell of food isn't far from here,
Full and bloated,
Back to the den,
Where you'll see the tiger rise again.

Armani Saintil (12)
St Peter's RC High School, Gloucester

A NAGGING PANTOUM

Why do teachers always nag you every lesson?
    Are you listening properly? Well look at me!
    Well how am I supposed to mark it? It's not here!
    Read the next paragraph! You should know where we are!

    Are you listening properly? Well look at me!
    You should know what to do by now, less talk more work!
    Read the next paragraph! You should know where we are!
    What is that supposed to mean? I've just explained it!

    You should know what to do by now, less talk more work!
    Any questions? No you can't, you've had all lunch break!
    What is that supposed to mean? I've just explained it
    No shouting out, you know you should put your hand up!

    Any questions? No you can't, you've had all lunch break!
    Do that again and I'll put you in detention!
    No shouting out, you know you should put your hand up!
    Are you chewing something? Spit it out this instant!

    Do that again and I'll put you in detention!
    Well how am I supposed to mark it? It's not here!
    Are you chewing something? Spit it out this instant!
Why do teachers always nag you every lesson?

Annie Copley (12)
St Peter's RC High School, Gloucester

THE CRY OF THE RAINFOREST

The tranquil rainforest lay peaceful under the moon's gaze,
Not a trouble in sight,
The night created an icy haze,
Soon the sun will reveal its light.

The many creatures awoke,
The green pastures of the rainforest revealed,
The stillness was broke,
Any wounded were healed.

Sounds, noises, brought immense fear,
Great evil lay ahead,
None remember the last tear,
Destroying until it's dead.

The end is close.
The cry of the rainforest can be heard far and post.

Chris Jones (13)
St Peter's RC High School, Gloucester

THE MOON

Yellow was the ball
When I saw her creep
Silently she rose
Into the night sky.

No bright star or cloud
Dares to block her light
Stars keep on shining
But cannot compare.

I feel very safe
When she shines on me
When she is shining
What is there to fear?

She brings me much joy
When the sun has gone
She keeps us so safe
That we can sleep on.

Joan Ashcroft (12)
St Peter's RC High School, Gloucester

THE ESKIMO

There was an old Eskimo who went to Peru,
Someone asked him, 'How do you do?'
'Do what?' the Eskimo replied,
'If you're talking about seals, I like them fried.'
The people of Peru were really astounded,
One boy said, 'I tried one once but I got grounded.'
The boy was standing in his pyjamas,
'After the seal I tried llamas.'
When the Eskimo heard this he laughed and laughed,
He said, 'You lot are really daft.'
He walked around town and went down to the beach
And there he heard an almighty screech.
It was a boat leaving for Rome,
He said to himself, 'I'm gonna go home!'
'But Eskimos don't come from Rome!' said the people of Peru,
The Eskimo replied, 'I do!'

Jack Breeze (11)
St Peter's RC High School, Gloucester

OPPOSITE CAT

Opposite cat,
Opposite cat,
Not a copy
But an oppy cat.
If I stand up really tall
He will curl into a tiny ball.
If I move to the left
He will move to the right.
If I move to the darkest shadows
He will move to the light.
If I go and sit in his basket
He will sit in my chair.
Even though he's a funny cat with his really spiky hair
He will be my oppy cat
Sitting over there.

April Jenner (11)
St Peter's RC High School, Gloucester

NEW LIFE

New life is the tide from the sea,
Sometimes far out, but you can reach it with a boat.
New life is your final destination,
You're weary when you arrive, but you enjoy it.
New life is the first cry, your first dream,
Don't waste life wishing it away.

It's a precious gift.

Elizabeth Davies (12)
St Peter's RC High School, Gloucester

IN DEATH'S SHADOW

The land was dusty and dirty,
People were helpless and dying,
There was a smell of fear in the air
And all I could hear was crying.

The people were just skin and bone,
Starvation was too much to bear,
They walked for miles to find food
And prayed there would be some there.

They searched the landscape for anything
That could lend them a helping hand,
But all they could see for miles and miles
Was stretches of empty land.

Fear of death all around them,
Flies crawling over their skin,
Too tired to think; too weak to cry,
Their emotions are kept deep within.

A baby lay dead by the roadside
Too weak to fight any more,
Her body lies putrid and broken
Upon the dry, barren floor.

The people had given up crying,
There was nothing more they could do,
Without any food and clean water
Soon they would be dead too.

Shannon Haigh (12)
St Peter's RC High School, Gloucester

DREAMS

Good dreams, bad dreams,
Many of a kind.
A good dream is happy,
A bad dream sticks in your mind.
A good dream makes you smile,
A bad dream makes you cry.
We all dream at sometime,
We dream what's on our mind.
No one likes bad dreams,
We like the good ones most,
So when we wake up in the morning
We can enjoy our piece of toast.

Lauren Bundy (12)
St Peter's RC High School, Gloucester

STARBRIGHT

Galloping around the woodland trees,
Frisking and frolicking in the autumn leaves.
I jump a log along the track,
My pony loves a long evening hack.
We get back and I give her a brush,
Her muddy coat goes smooth and lush.
Munching happily on freshly mown hay,
You could see my pony loved that day.
She nuzzles in close as I give her her oats and pat her goodnight,
My wonderful, wonderful starry *Starbright!*

Lindsey Browning (12)
St Peter's RC High School, Gloucester

THE BOY WHO NEVER SCORED

'To me, to me,'
He cries out loud.
'To me, to me,'
Hears the crowd.

'To me, to me,'
He wants the ball.
'To me, to me,'
They hear him call.

'To me, to me,'
They laugh out loud.
'To me, to me,'
They sound so proud.

'To me, to me,'
Still he shouts.
'To me, to me,'
Still laugh those louts.

'To me, to me,'
The gang approach.
'To me, to me,'
Now he cries, 'Ouch!'

'Not me, not me,'
They hit him once more.
'Not me, not me,'
Not now will he score.

Tom Hanley (12)
St Peter's RC High School, Gloucester

GUESS WHO?

Guess who?
Guess who?
I am
I am
Colourful and bright
Colourful and bright
Flying through the jungle
Flying through the jungle
All day and night
All day and night
Squawking with my friends
Squawking with my friends
Playing in the trees
Playing in the trees
You can keep me as a pet
You can keep me as a pet
But be careful what you say
But be careful what you say
I could repeat it some day.
I could repeat it some day.

Beccy Collinson (11)
St Peter's RC High School, Gloucester

CATS

Cats in the basket,
Cats in the garden,
Cats in the bathroom,
How'd you get there?

Cats in the car,
Cats in the kitchen,
Are you hungry
Kitty Kit Cat?

Cats on my lap,
Cats on the stairs,
When I turn around
Cats back in my chair!

Hannah Ahern (11)
St Peter's RC High School, Gloucester

THE NIGHT OF THE EARTHQUAKE

A shiver wavered through my spine.
My humoured body now dead with shock.
It came with no warning, but a definite sound,
As I lay in my lifeless bed.

The agony and fatal sound was killing.
Crash! Bang! Clatter!
Down went the photos, down went the door, down went the
Ornaments and then came the wall!

I lunged myself down the landing and sprinted down the stairs,
Along the hall dashing here and dashing there.
Out the front door I went to meet cries of help and pain.

What had I done, saving myself and not my loved ones?
I tried, I really did try to get back to the house but they wouldn't
                                                     let me in,
Said it was dangerous.
Said they'd get them, but they never did.

Rubble here, rubble there, rubble everywhere, all around me.
The sound had gone and so had my family, gone forever.
I shall never forgive that shapeless, faceless monster,
The nightmare of my dreams.
The . . . the
Earthquake!

Charlotte Withers (13)
St Peter's RC High School, Gloucester

SALTWATER

I sit here, eating fish and chips,
I smell the strong, sour, acidic vinegar.
I think about how this fish once swam in the colourful corals,
Swiftly weaving in and out,
Sharply darting, startled.

I sit here watching the waves
Crashing against the battered cliffs.
The fierce waves smash down the cliffs
Until there is nothing left but loneliness.

I sit here, watching the boats in the sea,
Bobbing up and down with the rhythm of the sea.
The sun is happily burning the backs of yachtsmen,
Whilst they concentrate on keeping their boats under control.

I sit here, watching the seagulls fly,
Soaring in every direction.
'Food, I need food!' I hear them say.
I scatter some chips across the floor.
The scavengers swoop down,
Now I have disappeared in a mist of gulls.

Jessica Jones (12)
St Peter's RC High School, Gloucester

DOLPHINS

Jumping, swimming in a blue-grey streak,
Shooting through the water as fast as the wind.
Friendly, chatty and very, very loveable,
Beautiful with their shiny, sleek, smooth skin.

Rebecca Shiers (12)
St Peter's RC High School, Gloucester

THE SPELL BOOK

Eye of newt,
Heart of an owl,
Feet of a hamster,
Cloth of a towel,
Head of a gorilla
And lungs of a killer.

Blood as fresh as can be,
Particles of elephant tea,
A hat just floating in the wind,
A tree that's silk and full of sap,
A mammoth's foot from the Ice Age,
A mammal inside a cage.

So when I read this magic book
I tried this spell upon the world.

Michael Smith (11)
St Peter's RC High School, Gloucester

THE TORNADO

The tornado has a powerful spin,
It tears up cities and trashes lives,
It destroys everything it comes across,
It has no feelings for its victims,
It has no gentle side!

Tom Wilkinson (12)
St Peter's RC High School, Gloucester

A STONE AGE POEM

We didn't have any transport
So everywhere we had to walk.
We only made grunts
Because we didn't know how to talk.

We lived in caves -
Nobody could build a house.
We ate what we could catch;
Sometimes only a mouse!

We could just about make tools
And used animal skins as clothes,
But the constantly moving around to catch animals
Is what everybody most loathes.

Only 20,000 years to go,
Then we develop into you
With electricity, computers and TV,
But never anything to do!

Charlotte Fox (12)
St Peter's RC High School, Gloucester

MAN

Staring through my window,
Sitting in a tree,
This little man always
Following me.

He has eyes as wide as oceans
That never blink,
Those eyes always
Follow me.

A little man about four feet two
His head and mine will never meet,
Hair black as coal,
Eyes dark as night,
The little man . . .

Alex Jones (11)
St Peter's RC High School, Gloucester

MY DAY

The sun sets about quarter-past six and the last of the light streams through the autumn trees.

I hear the cries of the mothers calling their children for dinner and the noise of the rush hour traffic rings in my ears.

The smell of dinner fills my nose, my empty stomach rumbles and my brain is working on my homework, like a clock; non-stop.

My bed calls for me after a hard day at school, and my room, my own special place, awaits me and my pyjamas feel soft and comforting.

I try to shut my eyes, but the bright streetlight pokes through my curtains, and the bright light of my alarm clock that shows at 10.30pm, streams into my half-open eyes.

My dreams are happy and colourful, my never-ending wishes; a happy world, a brighter future and mythical animal creatures!

The darkness of the night soon fills with the sunrise light, my eyes are now opened, and I can faintly see what now says 7.30am
on my alarm clock.

I now hear the buzz of the morning traffic and the school bus loudly beeps its horn, but I just stop and think for one minute that how lovely it is to have our world and all the beautiful things in it!

Gemma Hendzel (12)
St Peter's RC High School, Gloucester

KITTEN TROUBLE

I just can't sleep, I just can't rest,
These creepy-crawlies are trying to nest.

I itch and scratch, I just can't stop,
I think I'm going to lose the plot.

These humans, they don't understand
About the trouble the fleas have planned.

Down to my tail and then up to my neck,
They keep on going in their endless trek.

If you love and care for me so
Get the flea powder and make them go.

To thank you for your kindness shown
I'll curl up on your lap and show you how I've grown.

Melissa Davis (11)
St Peter's RC High School, Gloucester

MY DOG THE NONSENSE DOG

She's brown and white
And she does not bite.
She's got floppy ears,
She likes chasing deer.
She has a tufty belly,
She always turns out smelly.
I would not change her for any dog
Because she's my dog . . . Poppy.

Samantha Robertson (12)
St Peter's RC High School, Gloucester

AUTUMN TO WINTER!

Autumn advanced from the north,
As ever winter's scout preparing the way for the ice to come.
Winds charged at trees, tearing wildly at their green cloaks.
All too soon, the boughs hung their heads in despair,
Staring at the robes lying at their feet . . .
Once an emerald green,
Now a forlorn brown.
The small short grass as damp as ever, stays awake till winter arrives,
With its bag of frost and suitcase of coldness.
Trees do their chores like sweeping away the leaves with the wind,
But as the long hard working days become shorter,
The nice resting night to sleep in your bed becomes longer.

Amy Parkin (11)
St Peter's RC High School, Gloucester

TREE

Tree, tree, tree,
How big can you be?

They say you can be 80m tall,
Oh! You can be my wall!

Tree, tree, tree,
How long can you live?

They say you can live at least
2,000 years.

Oh! You're the biggest one of all!

Reanne Umali (11)
St Peter's RC High School, Gloucester

BY THE SEA

I watch a seagull in flight, as it ducks and dives through the posts of the pier hoping for a morsel thrown down from above by the happy, laughing, crying and moaning crowds above.
I want to join the hundreds who are making the noise of thunder
                                                    on wood.
The flashing lights of machines, the noise of the change as it hits
                                                    the metal scoop.

I wander outside and stare into the distance,
The salty sea air hanging around everywhere along the beach.
Strolling along the beach, my feet feeling as if they would sink
to the watery depths below, with the fish weaving in and out.
All the weeds and corals floundering around the bottom.

The cliffs at the end of the beach on their own with caves calling out to be explored, with huge stalactites hanging from the ceiling.
Water dripping with a *drip, drip, drip.*
Calm hanging around the region.

James Noble (12)
St Peter's RC High School, Gloucester

SALTWATER

As I walk along the beach
I hear the seagulls screeching
And the waves crashing on the sand,
Like the rain crashing on a stone-cold pavement,
Crash, crash.

I sit here, on the harbour, looking out
At a lonely boat drifting
And I see people with giant rubber rings
Floating slowly as if God was holding them
So they don't drown.

I pick up a rainbow of shells
And I walk slowly towards the sea,
Then I walk beside it, leaving footprints as I go
And then suddenly disappear
In a big wave.

Edel Quinn (12)
St Peter's RC High School, Gloucester

DESSERTS

Jelly, trifle, custard too,
Banana split and ice cream all for you.
Wibble wobble jelly,
Trifle on a plate,
Custard with banana,
Oh what a treat.
Banana split, yummy,
Ice cream runny,
Serve it all on a plate, doesn't it sound great?
Jammy biscuits,
Lollipops,
Lots of nice things to feed my chops.
Fairy cakes, yoghurt too,
Everything is chocolatey, wahoo!
Whoops-a-daisy I got it on my shoe,
Drip, drop lollipop,
Sticky, jammy biscuits,
The washing machines gonna have a feast.
Nice iced fairy cakes,
Sloppy, loppy yoghurt,
I hope it's not all pretend
I don't want this dream to end.

Hayley Dalley (11)
St Peter's RC High School, Gloucester

My Cat

My cat Toby makes me laugh,
He also makes me cry,
'Cause when I use a catapult
I really make him fly!

He likes to eat, he's really fussy,
In fact he's quite a pain,
If he doesn't get what he wants
He'll try and try again.

At first we called him Phoebe,
But alas, he was a boy,
So when we called him Toby
He miaowed out loud in joy!

Don't get me wrong or be confused,
I really love my cat,
No other pet could be better,
Not a rabbit or a rat!

Laurence Wilcock (11)
St Peter's RC High School, Gloucester

Vegetarians Are Evil

Vegetarians are mean,
They eat every bean.
Tomatoes don't stand a chance
To do the freedom dance.
Potatoes are baked or boiled,
Their life is definitely spoiled.
Vegetarians give vegetables no life
As they cut them all up with a knife.

Dominic Gray (11)
St Peter's RC High School, Gloucester

SALTWATER

I hear the distant squawk
Of flooding seagulls,
As they fish low above the surface of the water,
Better than any fisherman could ever be,
All joined together.

And then, the tide comes in,
The seagulls flee away,
The waves brush against the rocks
And crash back down.

And then silence, the water shut down
Like it wasn't breathing at all.

Daniel Sullivan (12)
St Peter's RC High School, Gloucester

ELEPHANTS!

Elephants,
Elephants plodding along,
Elephants,
Elephants grumbling and rumbling,
Elephants,
Elephants crunching and munching,
Elephants,
Elephants rolling and lolling,
Elephants,
Elephants sleeping and dreaming,
Elephants, shhhh!

Clare Aldred (11)
St Peter's RC High School, Gloucester

SALTWATER

As I sit here watching waves
Crash against the rocks,
I can hear the big blue boats
Battle against the waves
With the blood-red sky behind them.

        I sit and wait,
        Looking at the zesty sun.
        My cool creamy ice cream
        Decides to melt.
        Now I have a sandy
        Ice cream sundae.

The sandy, salty sea
Drags in slippery, slimy seaweed.
It strangles my feet, but I get loose
And the seaweed dies with the day.

Portia Costanza-Brown (12)
St Peter's RC High School, Gloucester

THANKING GOD

Thank you God for helping us all every day in our lives.
He helps people who need food and money.
He gives us good health and strength.
He saves those who are in danger.
He heals those who are sick.
He helps us in our studies too.
He gives us clothes to be warm.
O God, help us every day in our lives.

Steffi Saleem Sardar (11)
St Peter's RC High School, Gloucester

STAND AND STARE

I have no time to stand and stare,
People think the world is calm and peaceful,
But in my world it's different,
People don't know it but I will hunt them down
Because of something they did.

I have no time to stand and stare,
I'm always on the run,
Trying not to cause suspicion,
They don't know how hard it is.

I have no time to stand and stare,
Changing ID all the time,
Telling people things that I am not,
Telling lies that aren't forgotten.

When I have my gun,
I load it with ammo,
I go out to find my prey.

When I see the enemy,
I raise the gun,
I pull the trigger,
Now I'm on the run.

What happens can't be forgotten,
What has happened cannot be changed or replaced,
What has happened you must continue doing.

I am always on the run, what I cannot do is
    Stand and stare.

Gregory Henry (11)
St Peter's RC High School, Gloucester

SALTWATER

I lie here listening to the sea,
I think about how fish swim
In the colourful corals, weaving
In and out of the snake-like seaweed.

I look down at my sandals, I see
Them sink into the sand.
I start to stroll along the soft,
Warm bed it has formed.
I stop and look at the horse-like
Galloping sea, crashing.

I swiftly glide into the sea,
I can feel the slimy seaweed
Surrounding my skin.
I glance back and see some children
Building a sandcastle, happily.

There's a fisherman's boat
Far out to sea.
The egg-like sun is breaking,
The yolk shining.
I dive under the next galloping gang
And leave.

Lauradana Day (12)
St Peter's RC High School, Gloucester

THE WATERFALL

As the water drops, the magic of snow makes it white.
The moss is as green as grass and soft as cushions.
The rocks stick out at awkward angles.
Water dancing around the rocks, like at an ice rink.

Clouds making silly shapes, like a clown with balloons.
Two rocks sticking up at the death drop,
The rocks, making layers of slate
And the moss filling the gaps like cement.

Lawrence Jenkin (12)
St Peter's RC High School, Gloucester

SALTWATER

I sit here eating the catch of the day,
The strong fishy smell hovers in the air,
I think about how this fish
Once swam in the colourful corals,
Workings its way around the jagged rocks,
Sharply darting, startled.

I stand on the high rock looking down,
I see the waves crash against the rocks
Making the sea's surface frothy and white,
The waves soak the sand,
Leaving the sea's shore damp.

I amble down the lonely beach
With the sea splashing at my feet,
I see fishermen fishing in the harbour,
Wondering what to have for dinner.

I can smell the slimy seaweed in the cool sea air,
As the families who laugh and splash
Eventually get tired, the sea seems to feel the same,
So I sit and watch the sunset,
What an end to such a lovely day.

Lucy Church (12)
St Peter's RC High School, Gloucester

CASPER THE LION KING

My pussy cat of black and white,
Reflecting sun on eyes so bright.

Stretching in the morning sun,
You look so happy and full of fun.

Contentedly still on grass so green,
The best so far I've ever seen.

As you roll from side to side,
Your eyes light up so full of pride.

Reaching out to stroke his fur,
He shows his joy within his purr.

Through the trees the sun so bright,
Casper you are a true delight.

As he rolls and awaits my pat,
I know I've picked the perfect cat.

Gently playing, taking it all in,
You really are the Lion King!

John Lloyd Gardiner (12)
St Peter's RC High School, Gloucester

AFTER WORK

After work everyone's tired,
After work you like to lie down,
After work we go to the diner,
Drink, drink, drink.

In the diner a man walked in,
'Coffee,' he said to the barman.
The barman announced the very cheap price
And the man said, 'Yes, yes, yes.'

The man was there when a lady,
A lady with red hair walked in,
She sat there and sat there and sat there
Until her man walked in.

For a very long time they talked,
About many a thing they did,
Until the man lost his touch
And the lady got very bored.

Aleksander Konarski (12)
St Peter's RC High School, Gloucester

MY BEST FRIEND

We were like glue together,
nothing could get us apart.
We thought we would be best friends forever,
but then we fell apart.

I remember the way her face lit up when she saw me,
with a sparkle in her eye, like a diamond in the sun.
She ran like the wind as fast as lightning,
but we still had lots of fun.

I will never forget the years we spent together,
we would always have a laugh.
We had different personalities,
but that didn't matter we knew we would last.

But now she's gone and I'm still here,
I don't know what happened to us.
I miss her so she should come back,
someday, someday, someday.

Abigail Whitelow (12)
St Peter's RC High School, Gloucester

I Wish...

I wish I was a butterfly with blue wings like the sea,
Or maybe even a monkey to climb the highest tree.
I wish I was a giraffe and had the longest neck,
Or maybe even a chicken with the hardest peck.

I wish I was a crocodile that had the sharpest teeth,
Or maybe even a caterpillar that ate the greenest leaf.
I wish I was a polar bear with the whitest fur,
Or maybe even a cat with the loudest purr.

I wish I was a kangaroo that had the highest jump,
Or sometimes even a camel, which has more than one hump.
I wish I was a rat with the longest tail,
Or even a shell that sits upon a snail.

All these things I wish to be, cannot compare to the real me!

Harriet Walsh (12)
St Peter's RC High School, Gloucester

My Dad

His name is Russ,
He jokes and he smokes,
But his best quality is
He's a great bloke.

He played for Gloucester RFC,
Then he got a bit
Of an oldie.

On Sunday night he's quite boring,
In fact you can never stop him snoring.

Ross Ellis (12)
St Peter's RC High School, Gloucester

SALTWATER

I sit here watching the seagulls swoop through the sky
And watch the soft fluffy clouds float past.
I look at the clear blue sea, I watch small fish swim
In and out of the snake-like seaweed.
I watch crabs scuttle across the rocks like
They're in a hurry to get somewhere.

I look down at my sandals,
I see them sink into the sand,
I start to stroll along the soft
Warm bed it has formed.
I stop and look at the fierce sea,
Waves like horses galloping then crashing
Into cliffs nearby.

I walk along the harbour looking over
At the lonely hills so far in the distance.
I look at families sitting, children's joyful
Faces playing in the sand.
I look at the colourful yachts darting
Across the sea like a rainbow-coloured tide.

Then I walk over to the seaside market,
People in a hurry, buying their goods.
I smell fresh fish, the strong smell
That people hold their noses to.
Then I walk on ahead to the
Big crowd I see, then disappear
Into a tide of faces.

Yazmine Jackson (12)
St Peter's RC High School, Gloucester

THE OLD MAN

I stepped into the old, crumbling garage,
It was cold and dark inside and rats ran across the floor,
Dust clogged my nose,
I could hear someone breathing, a wheezy croak,
I took a step forward, did I dare go further?
My hands became clammy and bugs scuttled in my hair,
I carried on and there it was, a man leant against an old cupboard,
Groaning for help,
Who was he? Where was he from? So many questions came to me,
I stared at him, he was pale and slim,
His lips were blue and I could tell he was cold,
His grey hair stood on end and his knuckles were swollen,
I tried to think I was dreaming,
It couldn't be true,
I turned around and ran, I tripped as I came to the door,
Blood dribbled down my leg, I tried to wipe the tears from my eyes,
Would I see the man again?

Dawn Collins (11)
St Peter's RC High School, Gloucester

WINTER FALLS

Sweeping the ground the leaves settle,
The thorns are picking on the soft nettle,
The trees are standing there naked,
Branches bare for no leaves to stare.

Sliding up and down,
Children go laughing like a clown,
The ice cracking as they go,
The water will soon flow.

Snowballs flying here and there,
People being hit everywhere,
Snowmen standing there with eyes as black as coal,
The children's eyes shining bright,
Although inside there's a light.

Martin Micallef (11)
St Peter's RC High School, Gloucester

SALTWATER

I sit here, eating fish and chips,
I smell the strong, sour, acidic vinegar,
I think about how this fish once swam in
The colourful corals, swiftly moving in
And out, sharply darting everywhere.

I sit here, watching the sea,
Children pick up pretty pebbles and shells,
I get up, slowly moving towards them,
The scent of the sea gets stronger
While the sun digs deeper.

I sit here, the children have gone,
The sun has died, the moon is born.
My toes are tingling,
The tide is coming in,
Best be off to warm my toes.

I sit here just picking up my belongings,
I walk along the pier,
Watching waves and cliffs fight,
I find it hard to walk as my toes web together,
Winter trying to turn me into a seagull.

Esme Gibbons (12)
St Peter's RC High School, Gloucester

Saltwater

I lie here staring up at the cloudless sky, I can see
The sun setting and the moon awakening,
I think about how the Earth was once bare
And how it now shows great beauty.

I hear the distant squawk of the flooding seagulls
As they swoop low above the still surface of the water.
The fishermen watch
As they jealously lay down their nets.

I can see the waves fearlessly
Crashing against the open-face cliff,
Eager to push it aside with its mighty power,
Waiting for the cliff to edge away.

I walk along the beautiful golden beach,
I can smell the stench of rotten seaweed
Lying dead,
Dead as a sunken wreck.

David Hearfield (12)
St Peter's RC High School, Gloucester

My Grandad

I liked the way
He brought me sweets.
I liked the way
He cooked up meats.

I liked the way
He always cared.
I liked the way
He made me scared.

I liked the way
He was sometimes rude.
I liked the way
He got in a mood.

I liked the way
He larked about.
I liked the way
He pretended to shout!

Grace McAvoy (12)
St Peter's RC High School, Gloucester

STEPHEN PARSONS

S ee I am Stephen Parsons
T he day has come to tell you about me
E lizabeth is my sister's name
P arsons is my final name
H elen is my other sister
E xcellent at cricket, I am better than all the rest
N aughty prankster I am.

P ractising is what you need to do to get better and better
A dding, subtracting, dividing and timetables are what I like best
R acing is what I do not like
S tarting new games I like to do even if it takes all day
O n the ball that's me
N ow you know about me
S ummer is the best time of year.

Stephen Parsons (12)
St Peter's RC High School, Gloucester

ANGEL
(Based on Skellig by David Almond)

I saw an angel in my garage one Sunday afternoon,
I think it was because it was the day of the Lord,
I heard the heavens singing but he just snorted,
As he was ugly like a baboon,
Wicked like a witch.
Until one day I took him to a graveyard,
The heavens started singing again and all of a sudden,
He became as kind as an angel should be,
As gentle and soft as cats' fur,
And as beautiful as a new flower,
Some say I was dreaming,
Some say I'm insane,
But I know what I saw,
I know deep down inside it was an angel,
A kind,
Gentle,
Beautiful,
Singing,
Caring angel,
Sent down from the skies.

William Craig (12)
St Peter's RC High School, Gloucester

NIGHTHAWKS

All-night diner is what I sit in,
My feet tapping to the music from the jukebox,
My husband sitting next to me speaking about children,
I'm bored listening to him.

I can see the light shining onto the dark and lonely streets,
A man across the room staring at me,
Winks at me twice.

The man behind the bar
Whistling, while he gets me a strong whisky,
I'm sick of coffee,
Sick of life.

Lucy Reeves (12)
St Peter's RC High School, Gloucester

SALTWATER

As the fish gets swept away
By the waves crashing against
The rocky cliffs,
Leading the fish into a land
It does not recognise.

Then I look down
And see the sloppy sand
Swallowing my feet.
I look again and see
One, two, three, four, five fish
Swimming around my feet.
I throw a chip in and
All five fish swim to the top,
Fighting for it.

I watch for a moment,
Then look to see the time,
It seems all time
Is lost,
When I sit here
Eating fish and chips.

Lucinda Behan (12)
St Peter's RC High School, Gloucester

MY FRIEND CHAD

Remember that time,
The time when we had a dime?
Talking about girls
And their pearls.

Remember when we had a sleepover
And talked over and over?
Talking about brothers
And sisters.

Remember the parties
And all those Smarties
That went missing!

Remember Chad?

Sean McLoughlin (12)
St Peter's RC High School, Gloucester

SUNDAY MORNING

Sunday morning after a lazy lie-in,
I stumble down the stairs,
The smell of bacon clinging to the air,
Sleep still heavy in my head,
I run my hands down the banister,
My bare feet on the rough carpet,
The warmth of the kitchen window,
Only pure white snow stares back,
A shiver runs down my spine,
I could hear the wind whipping the leaves,
Thank goodness I'm inside.

Rebecca Holgate (12)
St Peter's RC High School, Gloucester

HALLOWE'EN WITCHES

I put on my hat and tie my cape tight,
Pull on my boots, I'm off for the night.

Pick up the cat and dust off the broom,
Out of the door with a whoosh and a zoom.

Up in the sky I now must fly,
I'm off to a party, I've no time to say hi.

I think its there, maybe it's not,
Oh deary me, I've dropped my pot.

There's the party, hip, hip, hooray!
It's nine o'clock, four hours to stay.

Aimie Moore (11)
St Peter's RC High School, Gloucester

SKELLIG
(Based on a book by David Almond)

I found him in the garage on a Sunday afternoon,
He had a pale and cracked face,
He was young, had black hair,
There were all dead bluebottles and spiders in the room,
He had all crooked wings and he is grumpy,
He was really smelly like he had never had a bath in his life,
It smelt like you were in a sewer,
There were lots of boxes with plaster on them,
It was disgusting, I would never go in there again,
In the end he flew away into the sky like an owl.

Nico Lanciano (11)
St Peter's RC High School, Gloucester

MY POEM
(Based on 'Skellig', by David Almond)

I found him in the garage that Sunday afternoon.
I could see walls crumbling, I walked in further,
In the corner was a marble fireplace crumbling terribly,
Behind the fireplace was a man.

I could smell the damp boxes, the dust, rotten beer and the stale
Chinese takeaways that the man had been eating.
I could taste the dust, as I walked closer to the man a lot of cobwebs
Were going into my mouth so I could also taste that.

I could feel damp Chinese takeaway boxes
And damp boxes with books in.
I could hear mice, spiders and bluebottles scurrying
Across the broken floorboards.

Sian Hopson (11)
St Peter's RC High School, Gloucester

MOSCOSKI THE SPY DOG

In the dark of the night,
Slinking from shadow to shadow,
Eyeing crafty cats that creep
And slink and disappear!

Moscoski's like an arrow,
Fast yet quiet.
Piercing the enemy,
They fall just like *that!*

In the dark of the night,
Slinking from shadow to shadow,
Moscoski is the best!
Fast . . . yet quiet.

Jessica Moore (11)
St Peter's RC High School, Gloucester

THE FIRE BELL

We were sitting in the class without a doubt
As the fire bell gave its frightful shout.
The children panicked, screamed and ran
Whilst the teacher called the fireman.
The school doors were opened wide,
Letting the children get outside
To somewhere safe, away from harm,
Away from the din of the fire alarm.
All of a sudden the brigade was here
To everyone's clap and cheer.
To our surprise an almighty noise,
'Move further away all you girls and boys.'
The flames, they were leaping in reds and blues,
By now our story had reached the news.
Suddenly - flames as tall as the sky
And children were worried, some started to cry.
The firemen battled and did what they could,
Though all that was left were some ashes and wood.
The firefighters worked with quite some pace
Whilst we all looked on with a sorrowful face
And as time passed and the flames they did quell
We all gave thanks for the sound of the fire bell.

Ben Kelly (12)
St Peter's RC High School, Gloucester

SKELLIG
(Based on book by David Almond)

I found him in the garage on a Sunday afternoon,
Dr Death never smiles, never laughs,
I wouldn't even go in there for danger money,
Bricks were crumbling,
Floor broken,
Dead bluebottles everywhere,
White face, black suit,
Skellig, Skellig, Skellig.
My heart thudded, thudded my heart,
Dreams, weird dreams,
Baby ill, very white face,
Pigeons hard as stone,
Aspirin, Aspirin,
27, 27, 27,
53, 53, 53,
Bossy, bossy, bossy,
Mina, Mina Leakey and Coot,
William Blake,
Remember shoulder blades are where
Your wings were!

Jade Turner (11)
St Peter's RC High School, Gloucester

LIFE IS COMING TOGETHER

Life is coming together
And we do not
Know what to do as
We waste away our planet.

Time is near the end,
We can't go on for much longer.
We're wasting
Away in sin.

Our lives are near the end,
What shall we do?
Our lives are near the end,
The killer is coming.

Michael Braicu (11)
St Peter's RC High School, Gloucester

SALTWATER

As the fish get swept away
By the waves crashing against
The rocky cliffs,
Leading a fish into a land
It does not recognise.

Then I start to walk
Along the broken cliffs and look far out
To the misty sea to watch the dolphins
Jumping in and out of the water
And then see all of the salty seawater sparkling
As they jump out and dive in.

Then as I see the water crashing against the rocky cliffs
I nearly slip on the cliffs but,
As I gently get my steady balance back
I see a couple of bright red crabs
Slowly walking against the cliffs
As if they have broken legs.

Then I take a slow walk to the beach path,
Going through the wet, rough sand,
Then through the soft, silky sand,
This makes my feet feel like I am walking through the air,
Then I smell the sweet, salty air.

Beth-Ann Davies (12)
St Peter's RC High School, Gloucester

TIGER BEGAN

He stole the creaking of a tree branch,
He stole the roaring of a stormy sea
And made his voice.

For his coat
He took the softness of a baby's cheek,
He took the orange of forest fruit,
He took the black of the ash from a forest fire.

From the black of the night
He snatched the silence of a creeping spider,
He snatched the movement of a fleeting shadow
For his walk.

Then at noon
Tiger snared the sharpness of a hunter's knife,
He snared the whiteness of an ivory tusk
To make his teeth.

Sharp leaves
Went into the curves of his eyes
And for their tone
He seized a flame of the burning sun -
And tiger was made.

Matt Davies (12)
St Peter's RC High School, Gloucester

SKELLIG
(Based on the book by David Almond)

I found him in the garage,
Weak, dirty, helpless.
The jagged mouth never smiled,
The crooked wings never flew.
When we moved him things changed.

In his eyes there was a twinkle,
A hint of a smile played round his mouth.
Stronger, powerful Skellig began to move.
At last, awakened, on his wings, he flew.

Harriet Anne Layhe (11)
St Peter's RC High School, Gloucester

THE USUAL STUFF

When I wake up tired, half sleeping,
Punch my alarm to stop it beeping,
All I think is,
The usual stuff.

When my lunch is cold and lumpy
And the dinner ladies grumpy
All I think is,
The usual stuff.

When darkness looms up to my bed
And I can't sleep, I can't keep the thoughts
Of terror from my head,
All I think is,
The usual stuff.

Why can't children rule the world?
Then fun and joy would be hurled
To every home.
Why can't our lives be free from school?
So we can banish all things cruel!
Like spelling tests and maths assessments,
But I alone can't make amendments
So I must stick to and nothing more,
The usual stuff.

Sacha Fullerton (11)
St Peter's RC High School, Gloucester

SEA AND SKY

Sea and sky, blue as can be,
I'm so happy when I go to the sea.
The sky always shines
And the sea glistens at me.
The sea gives me waves, the sun smiles at me!
When it gets dark
The stars come out,
The sea is so still
You can hear the fish scuttling about.
I felt the gentle wind blow sand in my face.
Sea and sky are having a race.
The sea has gone in, the sun has gone down!
It's time to go home as I'm all washed out!

Kerry Dooner (11)
St Peter's RC High School, Gloucester

SKATEBOARD

Baggy trousers, trendy shirts,
Four wheels, a board, let's get to work.
A few steps will do, a pavement clear,
In this game there's no room for fear!
The pavement makes a perfect jump,
But the neighbours they just seem to grunt.
They just don't seem to understand
Why this board is always in my hand.
I can't help thinking when at school
Those steps, that ramp,

My skateboard's cool!

Chad Kiely (12)
St Peter's RC High School, Gloucester

MY LIFE

In my house I lie on my bed,
Fall asleep and rest my head.
In the morning I have a bath,
Get changed ready for school,
Gel my hair so I look really cool.
I walk down the stairs
And play with my sister,
Leaving for school after having kissed her.
I run for the bus down the road,
Thinking my red face may explode.
Arriving at school in the bus,
Everyone shouting, what a fuss.
I have all my lessons with my friend,
At last the day finally ends.

Harry Lawlor (12)
St Peter's RC High School, Gloucester

MOONLIGHT

The moonlight shined and glistened onto the river.
The moonlight glistened on a bride in the darkness.
The moonlight shone in my window.
The moonlight shone on the trees.
The moonlight shone behind the hill.
The moonlight glistened in my face like a light.
The moonlight glistened into my sleep.

Damien John Walker (11)
St Peter's RC High School, Gloucester

ON HOLIDAY WHEN YOU'RE AT HOME

Summer is great,
When I say bye to all my mates.
It puts a smile on my face,
When I go and close the gate.

As I'm on the beach
You'll be eating a big fat juicy peach.
When I'm swimming in the pool,
You'll be thinking I'm really cool.

When I'm playing out in the sun,
It makes you want to run.
When I'm just leaving the beach,
You'll be thinking of a welcoming speech.

Emily Nash (12)
St Peter's RC High School, Gloucester

MY WINTER

My snowflake is unique and like no other,
It's cold like ice but fluffy like a feather.
It's beautiful; it stands out amongst all others,
But as I stand there gazing it melts and leaves me.
If only I could have one, just one so over the years I could
Remember this beautiful white winter.

Abby Collins (11)
St Peter's RC High School, Gloucester

ANIMALS

Animals are tall, round and small
I like animals of different kinds,
Those that swim, some may run and fall
And those that fly up so high.

Animals can be small furry things
Some with spikes, some with skin
Some with feathers, some with wings
And some with fins.

Animals like to eat
Some with spikes, some with skin
Some with feathers, some with wings
And some with fins.

Animals like to eat
So they can survive
Some eat veg, some eat meat
Just so they can fulfil their lives.

Animals live in many places
And do not like to show their faces
Most are shy, some are scared
Some might bite so be aware!

Shareena Toth (13)
St Peter's RC High School, Gloucester

They Can't Take It Away

They can do anything they want to do
They can say anything they want to say
Try to bring me down
But I will not allow
Anyone to succeed
Hanging clouds over me
And they can try hard to make me feel
That I don't matter at all
But I refuse to falter
In what I believe
Or lose faith in my dreams
Because there is a light in me
That shines brightly
They try
But they can't take that away from me
They can do anything they want to you
If you let them in
But they won't ever win
If you cling to your pride
And just push them aside
No
They can't take this
Precious love
I'll always have inside me
Certainly the Lord will guide me
Where I need to go.

Danielle Weir (12)
St Peter's RC High School, Gloucester

SPORT!

Sport is fun and good to do,
I like netball, hockey, basketball too.
It keeps you fit,
It keeps you healthy
And it could even make you wealthy.
Sport is what I choose to do
With my friends after school.
Better than being in my room
Watching TV all alone.
So come on everyone take the plunge,
Join a club and have some fun.

Robyn Fowler (12)
St Peter's RC High School, Gloucester

RAINBOWS

If you see a rainbow
Look high in the sky
See all the colours
Wonder what's on the other side?
Maybe a pot of gold
All your dreams come true
Flying through the sky
Smiling over the rainbow
I hope it's true
Sitting on a rainbow
That's what I dreamed to do.

Nuala Darke (12)
St Peter's RC High School, Gloucester

SILENT CONNECTION

We're all different,
Even if it's just the way we speak.
We all hurt in different ways,
Even if we say the same hurtful things.
Not everyone understands,
Even if we speak the same language.
Yet we all cry,
Even if tears fall in different colours

But it's not the way we speak or look.
What colour we are, or what language.
It's what's inside.
We are all one,
Just together in different ways.

Lianne Stimpson (15)
Thomas Keble School

EARLY MORNING NOISES

Birds going tweet with happiness,
Enjoying the rustling in the leaves,
Hearing the grasshoppers chirping,
The gentle wind rustling through the long breezy grass,
Streams trickling down the curves
And the little animals splashing water onto their faces.
Other than that completely quiet
But not forgetting the sizzling bacon going wild
In the kitchen.

Clair Gittings (12)
Thomas Keble School

CONFUSION

If life never involved any confusion would it be all that exciting?
Life would never have its ups and downs, its twists and turns, its issues.
It would be a straight roads to an empty highway.

You like this boy and he likes you but he has a girlfriend; confusion.
You put your diary down and you're sure it's in your desk
but it's actually in the bathroom; confusion.
You're going to the cinema with your friends
but have organised to go swimming with your cousin
at the same time; confusion.

If life never involved any confusion would it be all that adventurous?
Trying to get your head around how space goes on
for infinity; confusion.
Trying to pat your head at the same time as rubbing
your tummy; confusion.
Trying to say, 'Red lorry, yellow lorry' over and over again; confusion.

If life never involved any confusion would it be all that exciting?
Of course it wouldn't, life's one *big* confusion!

Louise Durman (15)
Thomas Keble School

BREAKFAST'S READY

The Rice Krispies go *snap, crackle, pop,*
The sausages *sizzle, sizzle, sizzle,*
The toast goes *crunch, crunch, munch,*
The orange juice glugs into the glass
Splish, splash, splosh,
The glasses bang down and the plates crash down
I bang down the stairs because breakfast is ready!

Katie Ponting (12)
Thomas Keble School

LATE NIGHT WALK DOWN THE RIDGE

Darkness is all around you,
Lights flashing through the windows.

No one is to be seen,
Apart from a little dog scrounging for food.

Then you see a car zoom along the road,
With the radio blasting at top volume.

Drunk teenagers coming home from the pub,
Shouting, with no care in the world.

People walking their dogs,
With torch lights shining.

The cold surrounds my village,
With only a few street lights to be seen.

The trees are rustling because of the strong wind,
A light flickers in the moonlight.

People are smiling with joy,
Delighted to live on this street.

Rachel Conboy (13)
Thomas Keble School

LATE NIGHT WALK DOWN TYLER'S WAY

Silence is all you hear
You see people walking around the homes

Lots of houses lit up like torches
And very few people walking their dogs

Next-door's dogs come back and yap
Her van drives up and she gets out

The yapping of those dogs stops
As the street lights flick on and off

Silence is what you hear
All you can smell is fresh air

The street is peaceful
Three doors down you see the TV flickering

As the trees rustle and
The smell is fine you walk down the hill smiling

So, as soon as you get into the house
You are happy to live in that street.

Ruth Fitzgerald (13)
Thomas Keble School

LATE NIGHT WALK DOWN KINGSCOURT

A lonely person in a Mini Cooper pauses.
The car engine is turned off.

A sudden rush of fear goes through his mind.
He suddenly turns the engine back on and drives off.

Trains speed along the tracks of the railway.

Birds tweet softly as if there is something silencing them.

A stranger walks down the subway into the glistening dark.

I walk down the subway as well
And see a tramp with a dog, snoozing.

The dog sat on a brown type luminous mat which looked weird.

The dog had a bowl next to its bed saying 'Fifo'.

James Thorburn (13)
Thomas Keble School

CHRISTMAS THROUGH AN OLD WINDOW

She walks up to the window and peers through the glass,
She sees her family at the perfect time of year.
She sees her mother baking Christmas cookies,
She sees her father putting up the tree.
She sees her elder brother helping her father,
She sees her younger brother pinning the stockings by the fire.

She pushes her nose against the glass and then pulls away,
She sees the very cold and wet pane of glass.
She sees droplets of water and condensation,
She sees mist from her warm, loving breath.
She sees snow being caught on the wooden window sill,
She sees it slowly gathering and building a small white mountain.

She looks into the pane of glass and her family disappear,
She sees a snowman in the background.
She sees her sledge ready and waiting on the floor,
She sees her reflection; it has changed an awful lot.
She sees wrinkles and grey hair instead of youth and sparkle,
She sees her past Christmas through an old window.

Hannah Baker (14)
Thomas Keble School

LATE NIGHT WALK DOWN ANGELICA WAY

Kids messing about on the road.
Their bike chains rattle.

A few houses with a shade of light.
I look over and listen.

Car doors bang.
A person puts the milk bottles out.

Tall buildings lean over the kids.
The kids are whistling.

A couple walk down through
The leant-over buildings.

I walked past a rusty car.
The dogs are barking.

I feel heat from the car bonnet.
The sound of sirens.

A man walks around.
Footsteps get closer.

Lauren Bain (13)
Thomas Keble School

LATE NIGHT WALK DOWN CHALFORD VALE

A stranger in an uptown car, stops beside a well.
His engine rumbles, as he waits.

A burst of anxiety rushes through the stranger's head.

In the distance, a woman walks down the street
Closely followed by her dog.

The dog sniffs the gleaming door of the Peugeot 206
As the stranger still waits.

The woman passes without the dog
Who is still sniffing at the door of the 206.

As the woman edges away, the stranger jumps out
And as quick as a flash, pulls the dog inside.

The stranger opens a box in the car.
It contains his mother's dog's food.

A light flickers on as the stranger feeds the dog
And the dog licks him. He was the stranger's dog all along.

Rob Rogers (13)
Thomas Keble School

LATE NIGHT WALK DOWN CRANHAM STREET

I was walking down Cranham Street,
When my sister's boyfriend drove past with his radio booming.

I carried on walking down the long and windy road,
Until a policeman pulled up and asked me what I was doing.

The police went so I carried on walking,
But then I looked into the woods and I saw two men smoking.

I ignored them and carried on walking until
I was opposite the Black Horse pub where I heard drunk
people singing.

I went inside and had a drink or two,
When I came out it seemed darker but I carried on walking.

Then I came across a woman carrying a pig,
I shouted, 'Give me that pig and I'll eat it for you.'

I was getting really bored of walking by now,
But I knew it wasn't much further to go.

Then I saw it. I saw my mate's house,
So I went inside and we started partying.

Christopher Job (13)
Thomas Keble School

YET THE NIGHT SEEMS SILENT . . .

The trees are rustling,
The owls are hooting,
The birds are tweeting
And yet the night seems silent . . .

The bugs are buzzing,
The guttering is dripping,
The rabbits are nestling
And yet the night seems silent . . .

Lisa Rice (12)
Thomas Keble School

LATE NIGHT WALK DOWN FAR OAKRIDGE STREET

A fastrack whizzing round a sharp corner
and it has a big headlamp.

Two super cars zooming down my street
doing dragster starts, like spinning wheels.

A really smelly, smelly dustbin sitting on the lawn
doing nothing.

The door of a fastrack, it is smooth and
has lots of shiny glass.

Lights going out,
porch lights turning on.

Two JCBs in a field,
ploughing and seeding.

A really big smelly muckspreader going down to the farm,
dropping muck on the road behind him.

Some large railings on the way to my house,
really, really cold.

Daniel Rotter (12)
Thomas Keble School

LATE NIGHT WALK DOWN BURLY STREET

A pack of townies talk, smoke and laugh at the end of the street,
an owl hoots and flies into the night

Some people come out of the all night ice cream parlour,
called D&Gs, at the opposite end

They walk past them, exchanging glances
and disappear into the darkness

The yellow street lights attract a load of midges,
water drips steadily from a broken pipe

The townies are standing by a pub,
the owner comes out and tells them to go

They all go their separate ways,
two walk down the street and go into D&Gs

Two skaters come into Burly Street,
They can barely walk

At one o'clock, the deep throbbing of music starts up,
The street is bare, dark and bleak.

Dave Brook (13)
Thomas Keble School

LISTEN MR HEAD TEACHER

Listen Mr Head teacher
I have a big problem
With ya uniform
It's 'orrible.

I think we should wear none
Like what we want
Children hate it
Change it for the kids' sake.

When I took it to Sir
He looked at it and said,
'I hate this idea
And if I could I would shoot you!'

Mr Head teacher didn't like it
He left the next day
So kids beware if you ask for a uniform change
You could get threatened.

Daniel Browning (12)
Thomas Keble School

LATE NIGHT WALK DOWN MUTTON LANE

A car goes down the lane at high speed,
lights on and music blaring.

Birds and other animals make lots of noises
in the dark woods by my house.

The moon shines bright in the sky. So do the stars
and then I see Steve walking up the lane with his dog.

More cars go down the lane and then I hear some arguing
coming from the house next door.

I continue walking down the lane and then in front of me
I see a fox run across the road into the bushes.

Then I hear a car coming up the lane. I stand on the side of the lane.
I see the driver with a fag in his mouth.

I walk further and see a light coming towards me.
It was bright as it came closer. I saw it was my dad's friend Mike.

I walk back to my house talking to Mike about school and football.
Then I get home and do my homework.

Edward Parsloe (14)
Thomas Keble School

BREAKFAST

Coming down the stairs in a daze,
There I was amazed,
The sound of my brother's cereal pop,
The gulp when he swallowed the loops,

There was Mum in the corner munching toast,
She said she was cooking a roast,
I heard my bacon sizzling in the pan,
The heat gave me a tan,

Dad was sitting at the table ripping the bill up,
There goes my pup,
Bang of her tail on the door,
I made her lie on the floor,

I sat down at the table,
Here comes Hazel,
Mum placed my bacon and beans in front of me,
I know where I must be.

Josie Fowler (12)
Thomas Keble School

THE WRITER OF THIS POEM!

The writer of this poem is as fast as fast can be,
Forgetful as a fish,
Hungry as a hippo,
Lazy as a cow,
Lively as a kangaroo,
Sleepy as a bear in winter,
As happy as a clown.

Tom Prosser (12)
Thomas Keble School

READ THE NOTICE!

Work in progress!
Please knock!
Wipe your feet!
Password incorrect!
Beware of the dog!
Get lost!
Fire door, keep shut!
Enter at your own risk!
Access denied!
No door to door salespersons!
Go away!
Do not disturb!
Silence please!
Trespassers will be prosecuted!
Private!

Brighid Nathanson (13)
Thomas Keble School

WHAT TO CALL A DOG

Bad biter
Bone hider
Big barker
Grumpy growler
Hole digger
Hungry hunter
Postman scarer
Tail wagger
Teddy tearer
Toy snatcher.

Stella Watts (12)
Thomas Keble School

PEOPLE

The wickedness of what the window reveals is haunting,
The masses of people within an inch of their lives
The way other people run after them
Is so annoying.
They are only just alive.
They must just want to be left alone.
Wouldn't you?
Then ill people must feel more invalid than they already are.

My breath steams up the window,
The droplets of condensation stream down the window.
The smeary lines where the window has been wiped before
Covers up the pane.
The smell of disinfectant
Taints the air.

As I look into the glass it reflects my face.
I see wrinkly lines.
Each wrinkle, each line, seems new to me.
As I look harder I see an old woman staring back at me.
It seems like thirty years have passed,
Without me noticing at all.
I see the bed behind me and realise that
I am one of those people too.
I am in a hospital,
We are all in a hospital.

Camilla Allan (13)
Thomas Keble School

MURKY WATER

The last day of the school year,
Gonna paddle in the murky water of Weston.
Allowed to soak the summer dress,
Nothing unusual about today.
There I am playing with my elder sister,
In sight of my mum.
Then it goes wrong!

Finding the edge of the boat run,
I slip!
The water over my head,
I can't swim,
Seaweed grasping me,
Pulling me down,
My lungs are going to explode,
I gasp in vain,
I am lost!

I find myself being pulled out of the water,
It's my older sister,
She has saved my life!
Walking back to Mum in tears,
Everyone staring at me,
They didn't help.
A big hug from my mum.
I am safe!

Felicity Venning (15)
Thomas Keble School

WAR THROUGH A WINDOW...

All I see, everywhere I look,
Are the lives people stupidly took,
I see pain, suffering and death
Worldwide destruction, not anything less.

When will these clouds of destruction clear?
Shooting and killing is all I hear,
When will the world finally see,
That war is not the answer you see.

It's not fair on the people who are still young,
The people whose lives have not yet begun,
What is the point of having a war?
You can't solve issues with killing and gore.

Miranda Love (13)
Thomas Keble School

TIGER

Deer chaser
Jungle ruler
Noisy roarer
Grass creeper
Dog growler
Hungry prowler
Noisy growler
Human eater
Man hunter
Meat muncher
Stripy danger.

Jonathan Weaver (12)
Thomas Keble School

THE WINDOW

I stand and look out of my window,
I see snow, lots of snow,
I also see fairy lights and tinsel,
I suddenly realise that it's Christmas,

As I stare out of the window I see
Snowflakes, dead bugs and
A spider's web made out of silk
With tiny droplets of water that look like diamonds on it.

As I gaze out of the window,
I see the reflection of a girl,
She has long brown hair and deep brown eyes.
She has a smile on her face, with a twinkle in her eye.
As I stare at the reflection I realise the girl is me.

Heather Wood (13)
Thomas Keble School

CAR

Horn blower,
Fast racer,
Old banger,
Race winner.
Speed breaker,
Cop racer,
Car crash,
Wheel burner,
Road runner,
Scary driver,
Road rage
Car wrecker.

Daniel Weston (12)
Thomas Keble School

WORLD WAR

I look out of the window and see devastation, hearts broken,
I'm standing here in my house, everyone is rushing around,
I just stand and stare and look upon the damage that has been caused,
I'm staring outside to world war.

I see on the window blood from people dying,
I see a mixture of black smoke and dust smeared on the window,
I see a cobweb in the corner as calm as can be,
Time seems to be frozen.

I gaze deeply into the window,
Then I see a girl standing there with emerald eyes looking sad,
The girl looks frozen and in a deep daze,
The lights are flickering, I'm frightened.

Will I live?

Emma McCartney (13)
Thomas Keble School

LIZARDS

Fun walker
Eyes changer
Smart thinker
Skin peeler
Colour changer
Sun beater
Beetle muncher
Hawk eyes
Fruit snatcher
Habitat hinder
Tongue twister
Lively licker.

Tom Jones (12)
Thomas Keble School

ALERT 5

'Launch the Alert 5 aircraft!'
'Take off immediately to clear the flight line!'
These voices were ringing out over the microphone, constantly
barking orders from the tower.
I looked out at the view from the canopy.
Three planes and a couple of badgers,
All being pelted with rain from the shattered grey skies.
Stretched out before me was the runway and the dark ocean.

The rain got more violent suddenly as a wave hit the carrier,
It struck the ship with tremendous force.
Water ripples came down the glass,
Blurring the picture that I saw.
There were scratches on the surface,
As if a tiger had run its claws across it.
A distant clunk of the blast deflector hit my ears.

I looked dead ahead, the flashing controls,
They were blinking like a Christmas tree.
I saw a face on the HUD.
A dark mysterious face with black eyes,
He had a sinister look about him,
His helmet covered most of his face
And then suddenly I realised,
It was me.

Although my mind was elsewhere,
I was throttling up.
Blazing heat at the back of the plane,
The plane being held back wanting to be let go.
They released me,
And the thrust pushed my plane and me,
Into the dark grey clouds.

Theo Durrant (13)
Thomas Keble School

KENNINGS

Milk lapper
Lazy sleeper
Loud purrer
Slow runner
Enjoys beating
Sharp clawer
Likes eating
Hates water
Mouse chaser
Dog fearer
Street fighter
Friend maker
Leg rubber
Fly carrier.

Ross Collins (12)
Thomas Keble School

SOME DAY

Some day I'll be treading on the green grass beyond the fence.
Some day I won't be lying on a hard bed.
Some day I won't have to look at the plain walls.
Some day I'll be sitting by my warm fire.
Some day I'll get to see my son.
Some day I'll kiss my wife's warm face.
Some day I'll be flying again in the clear blue sky.
Some day this war will be over.

Joshua Hale (12)
Thomas Keble School

What I Love Best!

The thing that I love best is going out.
I enjoy skiing down a slippery slope
And falling down badly without a doubt!
I like a bath with lots of bubbly soap.

I love seeing a film at the cinema.
My television is never turned off!
I like to go round and see my grandma.
I enjoy shopping, but not with a cough!
I love playing on PlayStation 2s.
Music is a nice thing to listen to.
I read magazines, but not on the loo!
I like to spend money and have something new,
So going out is the thing that I love best,
Because it is above all the rest!

Leah Cratchley (13)
Thomas Keble School

Lizard

Fruit snatcher
Funny walker
Smart thinker
Tongue twister
Habitat hider
Skin peeler
Colour changer
Sunbather
Tongue extender.

Jonathan Brown (12)
Thomas Keble School

WINDOW

Looking through the window,
What do I see?
People tossing and turning,
In their resting place.
Flowers, wilting and dying,
Like the people below.
Looking through the window,
What do I imagine?
People waking and rising,
From their resting place.
Flowers, growing and turning black,
In their vase of blood.

Looking at the window,
What do I see?
Flies, tangled in cobwebs,
Waiting to be freed.
Spiders, returning to feed,
Sucking the blood from the victim.
Looking at the window,
What do I imagine?
Dead flies, buzzing and flying,
Trying to escape.
Spiders, returning with fangs,
To suck the blood from the living.

Looking at the window,
What do I see?
Myself, pale and white,
Wanting and waiting to go.
Sweat, dripping off my forehead,
Collecting on the sill.
Looking at the window,
What do I imagine?

Something coming, what is it?
It's pale and coming.
I scream, but cannot move,
It's gone, where is it now?

Katherine Warner (13)
Thomas Keble School

LATE NIGHT WALK DOWN WHITEWAY

A poodle walked through the night,
Looking for food.

Through the dark night he finds food,
No light shines.

The smell of food,
And the sound of laughing roams the air.

The touch of the cold wind wraps around the houses,
With the taste of fresh air.

A baby cries to keep everyone awake,
Lights going on and off.

Then silence. Nothing has happened.
Suddenly, a light goes out.

The lights and TVs turn off,
Everyone has gone to sleep.

The village has died down.
It's got so cold.

Georgina Bullough (13)
Thomas Keble School

HEDGEHOGS

Winter sleeper
Night crawler
Warm hearted
Prickly spiker
Leaf eater
Mud mover
Twitchy nose
Leaf roller
Slug muncher
Warm slurper
Beetle cruncher
Bug sniffer
Leaf shuffler
Eye twinkler.

Becky Short (13)
Thomas Keble School

SHOES

High heels clicking down the hall,
A young child's boots, very small.
Splashing in the rain in wellies,
Playing near the sea in jellies.
Sandals padding over the grass,
Don't dare to wear trainers into class.
Flip-flops pushing through the sand,
Lace-ups with a thin band.
Take your pick,
Cos they're all chic.

Rhiain Nathanson
Thomas Keble School

IF I COULD WALK

If I could walk I could reach a shelf up high.
If I could walk I could look people in the eye.
If only I could play football,
I would feel ten feet tall,
But I can't so that's that.

If I could walk I could do more work.
If I could walk I'd go berserk!
If only I could ride a bike,
That's what I'd really like
But I can't so that's that.

If I could walk I could wash the car.
If I could walk I'd drive a sports car.
If only I could afford a sports car,
That's what I'd really like,
But I can't, so that's that.

If only I could walk!

Matthew Dean (17)
Thomas Keble School

TWISTER!

T hunderbolt through the dark sky
W inds blowing harder and stronger.
I ce falling, wind and rain whipping across my face
S mashing everything that gets in its way
T hunder claps overhead
E verything moving, spinning and turning
R ooftops tossed, houses crashing.

Emma Townsend (12)
Thomas Keble School

THE DONKEY

I wanted to be Herod
Herod had the biggest part
Why me?
Why do I have to be the donkey?
The donkey had to carry the heavy load on its back.
Hannah was Mary.
She was the heavy lump.
I struggled along
Towards a crowd of people,
A crowd of people that stared.
The sweat fell into my eyes.
The wool-like costume itched my skin.
I tried to hold my nose,
Matthew was very smelly.
Why do I have to be the back of the donkey?

Luke Nash (16)
Thomas Keble School

WORK IS...

The strain of getting up at six in the morning,
The terrifying light-speed drive when you're running late,
The annoying moan from your boss when you arrive half an hour late,
The horrifying pile of paperwork put on your desk,
The minuscule four weeks off a year,
The dragging-on overtime to get work finished,

The rewarding pay packet at the end,
The relaxing weekend,
The long awaited Christmas bonus at the end of the year.

Simon Brown (14)
Thomas Keble School

WHAT TO CALL A DOG

Toy fetcher
Fast runner
Fur moulter
Animal chaser
Fly eater
Wasp catcher
Postman biter
Stranger attacker
Floppy-eared bouncer
Sharp teeth shredder
Clever thinker
Skin licker
Skin biter
Cat killer.

Shane Rowles (12)
Thomas Keble School

WHAT IS THE MOON?

The moon is a sack forming seeds of light
The moon is a biscuit that has been bitten in half
The moon is a lighthouse in the background
The moon is a flashlight in a dark house
The moon is a boomerang thrown far away
The moon is a bow and arrow shooting out light
The moon is a bomb exploding out light.

Mitchell Tudor (11)
Thomas Keble School

WASHDAY CAROUSEL

Spin, slip, spin, slip
Clothing carousel
Cotton horses parade around
Wet beads shake off their tails

Roll up, roll up
Well, come on inside
There's no fee, it's all free
Garments only may ride

Trot on, trot on
It's time for one last go
Toss your manes before it rains
And the curtain falls on the show.

Sarah Finch (15)
Thomas Keble School

HORSE

Racing galloper
Mane shaker
Radar ears
Fast walker
Cross-country winner
Bumpy trotter
Big jumper
Pillow stuffer
Tail swisher
Hay consumer
Loud neigher
Smooth canter
Good dressage.

Philip Buckle (12)
Thomas Keble School

LEAVING HOME

It is a time everyone will go through,
It is a time that some look forward to,
It is a time that some will dread,
It is a time some have no choice about,
It is the time of leaving home.

It is a time of sadness and glee,
It is a time that in truth
Can be scary,
It is a time of change,
A time of freedom,
A time to spread your wings,
It is the time of leaving home.

To have a place of your own,
To set your own house rules,
To be who you want to be,
To express yourself happily,
You could even paint the whole place black!
It is the time of leaving home.

So feel good to go,
You've done well so far,
Now show the 'big bad world' what you're made of,
Pack your stuff,
So say farewell,
But not goodbye,
You will soon be back to get your washing done.

Dan Flack (15)
Thomas Keble School

SONNET

Bruises and cuts all over her body
Has she been abused since she was little?
Being so vulnerable
At least she hasn't been belittled.

She went through so much pain
No one there to help her
She had nothing left to gain
She decided to buck up and be brave.

Getting to a stage where she was
Continually being scared
Why does it keep going on?
She has taken all she can bear.

This has gone on so long, she's fading away
Why can't it stop? She's longing to stay.

Lindsey Bentall (15)
Thomas Keble School

NORTHERN OBSERVATIONS

Look at 'er o'er there
God, she's bloomin' mardy
Never a smile,
Just a blog on
Permanently affixed upon her face

Look at 'im, I bet he's single
What's he up to now?
Touched that's what he is,
With a sweater like that
He's moon-kissed

Ooh! That were a mistake
She's too old and flabby
Pink, stretchy with sequins
Ouch, not flattering

What's tha' lookin' at?
Nowt wrong with me.
It's rude to stare, to judge
I'm just people-spotting!

Katy Costigan (15)
Thomas Keble School

THE SILENT ROOM

As the silence in the room,
A lonely child holds a broom,
Tired from the day's work,
It makes its way home,
Passing office of the clerk.
The single sound of the phone.
The phone now answered, the child
hesitates.
Clerk says, 'No, I'm alone.'
'I must go now,' the clerk now states.
From all the dust lain around,
The child suffocates.
Falls down dead.
Clerk heard a thump, came out and said,
'This plum child banged its head!
What shall I do?'
Checked the pulse,
'Condolences seem due.'

Kirsten Webb (13)
Thomas Keble School

WHY DID THIS HAPPEN TO ME?

Why did this happen to me?
My life feels like a train
Whizzing past in the bleak, grey rain
Chugging past everything happy
And stopping at all the bad bits.

Why did this happen to me?
I feel like crying all the time
It feels like the sun will never shine
Not in this part of the world anyway
Not where I stand.

Why did this happen to me?
No one seems to notice my despair
They just stand and stare
Too busy with their own problems
I deal with mine alone.

Why did this happen to me?
It feels like there's no way out
I want to scream and shout
But the darkness chokes me
I'm unable to breathe.

Why did this happen to me?
Everyone gets these points in life
Feeling like they've been stabbed with a knife
It will get better one day
The pain will go away
It's never there to stay.

But why did this happen to me?

Holly King (15)
Thomas Keble School

THE COMMAND

Tick-tock, tick-tock,
As I sit squinting my eyes from the back row,
Through my dark glasses, a sunset drowning.

The rusting of the steel settling on the chairs
And the markings of others, engraved deep.
My head rises and I gaze across the flowing fields,
But first through the marked window of Class 3.

Snap! As a bag of bones clip past my face,
I jump back into my body
And my eyes are glued to my faithful teacher
Who's hovering in front of me
Like a dragonfly in distress.

Still my head fills up with anger and embarrassment,
But I think of her trying to teach us
And her knowledge of her travels.

The screeching of chalk, down a black mountain,
With the language of which I don't understand.
Through the sparks of my brain,
Quick ideas shoot like a stalk.

In my mind I know I can do
Everything that is needed in this world!
So I wipe my glasses for a second time
And realise, the world which surrounds me,
I see a better view.

Kelly Clark (13)
Thomas Keble School

QUESTIONS

Who knows what life holds for us?
What joys, what sorrows fate has planned for us
And when it's ending, who will cry for us?
And die for us?
And when we're down, who will fight for us?
When hope is gone, what is left to save us?
When faith is gone, who is there to pray for us?
And when we die, who is there to say goodbye for us?
And when our strength has gone, who is there to try for us?
And when we know all there is, who is there to ask for us?
And when we are happy, who is there to laugh for us?
And when all our dreams are answered, who will dream for us?
And care for us?
And share our sorrows for all that we have lost?

Saskia Stainer-Hutchins
Thomas Keble School

WHAT IS THE MOON?

The moon is a grey spark
shot into space.

The moon is a silver kite
flying high in the sky.

It is a bullet
shot into black blood.

The moon is a headlight
splashed on a dark wall.

The moon is a white, metal ball
kicked in a winter's night.

Sam Underwood (11)
Thomas Keble School

A Student's Arranged Marriage

Homework is like an arranged marriage.
Planned, prepared and pressured onto you when decided by your folks.
There is no way out. No escape. Nothing.
I suppose there are the excuses, but few of them work.
'My dog ate it'. No food going then?
'I left it on my desk'. Where were all of the other pieces of work then?
Excuses do you no good. Once you have it, that's it.
You've now realised that all of tonight's plans are ruined.
You know it will take time. You know it will mean effort.
You know it will actually need some thought.
To be honest, mate, you're doomed.
But hey! Look on the bright side!
It gets you out of the chores! Perfect!
Oh what's the point? Homework's always going to tie you down,
Stop the fun, shatter the freedom.
Just like an arranged marriage.
I guess you'd better start counting those days . . .

Ashley Birkin (14)
Thomas Keble School

What Is The Moon?

The moon is a giant balloon in the black sky,
A silver milk bottle top on a dark blue piece of paper.
An apple pie in a black dish.
A silver coin on the floating sea.
A crystal ball on a black piece of silk.
The moon is a shining wrapper in a black bin bag.

Stephanie Nash (11)
Thomas Keble School

A Walk Down My Road (Late At Night)

A miaow as the cats come out
A flash of red and white as a fox darts away.

The murmur of people talking, TVs playing
Cars drive past, stereos blaring.

People gather at the bench at the bottom
A yellow light shines on them but they cover their faces.

Lights start to turn off, bonfires start blazing
A party starts over the road.

The fountain closes, people go home
Teenagers, adults sing up the road.

People start to wake and stir
Rebels go; peace at last.

Silence now, but not for long
Someone, something will stir it soon.

Bonfires die down, the party's finished
The road's silent, it will start again tomorrow.

Eleanor Seager (13)
Thomas Keble School

What Is The Moon?

The moon is a bottle of milk floating in the calm, blue sky
It is a 10p coin dropped down in a bucket of white paint
It is a white football kicked up high in the dark sky with floodlights on
It is a torch shining in the dark sky
It is a white biscuit bitten in half.

Craig Stephens (11)
Thomas Keble School

A Poem About Sara Sharp

S ara is my name,
A lways doing something creative,
R eading is my favourite thing,
A rt is my best subject at school.

S itting is something I can't stand,
H ave always got mates to hang around with,
A lways love a bit of nature,
R ather annoying, I must admit,
P eople always like me, though.

I love to do outdoor stuff as well as in,
S tarting to grow up a bit now.

G ardens are so boring, out in the street is better,
R iding a bike is one of my hobbies,
E ating is a great thing to do,
A friend to all.
T K is a great school.

Sara Sharp (11)
Thomas Keble School

What Is The Moon?

The silver moon is a shining silver plate in the black sky.
It is a silver coin dropped down into Heaven's sky.
It is a shining screw drilled at the bottom of a shoe.
It is a silver cup, drinking water out of it.
The moon is shining like a bright star in the black sky.

Ann-Marie Hands (11)
Thomas Keble School

LATE NIGHT WALK DOWN BLUEBELL RISE

An owl flies, lands and shrieks,
then flies off into the dark abyss of the night.

Empty cars are parked with alarms turned on,
any movement and they will scream.

A street light twinkles over the pavement
but the moon is full and lights up this part of the world.

A car starts up, speedily reversing down the drive,
around the corner and down to the main road.

On down around the corner to where all the kids play,
and into the cats' territory.

Cats are the bosses down here,
but you can still hear dogs barking from houses.

We keep on going until we're near the road,
but the noise is much greater than at the top.

At the main road, a motorbike zooms by,
off into the distance.

Stuart Austin (13)
Thomas Keble School

WHAT IS THE MOON?

The moon is a ball of snow falling from the sky.
It is a pint of milk going into someone's mouth.
It is a white football being whacked into the white net.
It is a white piece of paper in a dark drawer.
It is a trainer which is as new as a small apple.
The moon is a ball of snow disappearing.

Laurie Merchant (11)
Thomas Keble School

WHAT I DESIRE

I've been up worrying all night,
I pray this interview goes right.
A job in commercials is just up my street,
Me in an advert about a bubble spa for feet.
I have worked in retail, that's finished and done,
Being an actress is much more fun.
I took drama at school and got an A,
What a great start to being famous one day.
My name is now called and it's time to go in,
So wish me luck, a new career could begin.

Watch this space!

Kerry Brown (14)
Thomas Keble School

WHAT IS THE MOON?

The moon is a silver milk bottle top
that has been thrown up into the sky.

The moon is a silver spotlight
that covers the sea.

The moon is a silver plate
in a dark cupboard.

The moon is a silver spaceship
flying through the dark sky.

The moon is a massive snowball
falling through the sky.

Chris Lees (11)
Thomas Keble School

My Late Night Walk Down Sheep Street

As I walk along the side of the main road,
Two motorbikes whizz by and go down Sheep Street.

I turn down Sheep Street and listen,
An argument rages, loud shouts all around.

As I get closer I can hear what they are saying,
They argue about noise from each other's houses.

I pass the arguments and it sounds like mumbles,
All I can hear is the owls hooting.

I hear a noise getting louder and louder,
I can see what it is, it is the two motorbikes again.

All is quiet again and all I can see is a lone street lamp,
The street lamp marks the end of Sheep Street.

I walk closer to the street lamp,
I see smaller lights whizzing by, they are cars.

I get close enough to hear the cars well,
I then turn down Lamb Street.

Richard Montague (13)
Thomas Keble School

What Is The Moon?

The moon is a pound coin in a purse.
It is a pebble dropped in a puddle.
It is a silver ring on a lady's hand.
It is a silver coin printed on a black dustbin bag.
It is a silver palm touching a ball.

Jamie Goode (11)
Thomas Keble School

LATE NIGHT WALK DOWN BISLEY OLD ROAD

A 50-year-old man with a cap and shades walks down the road,
A cigarette burning in his hand.

A drunken young lady with blonde, flowing hair, stumbles across
                                                                         the road,
Fumbling with her key in the lock.

The 50-year-old man stops to stare
And mutters something under his breath.

The woman hears and stops,
She stumbles forward and throws a punch, but misses and falls
                                                                          on the damp floor.

He pulls her up by the arm and shouts abuse in her face
And he hits her hard, with his already bruised knuckles.

She screams in pain, but he hits her more
And tells her to, 'Shut up and get inside!'

Lights in other houses flash on,
The man runs.

A policeman arrives and helps the lady up,
'It was my husband,' she whispers in fright.

Clair Akhurst (13)
Thomas Keble School

WHAT IS THE MOON?

The moon is a silver diamond on a ring.
It is a bottle lid shining in the sun.
It is a silver car sparkling in the light.
It is a piece of metal on a piece of black paper.
It is a silver coin in a dark cupboard.

Michael Ryan (11)
Thomas Keble School

DEATH BY FIRE

A rumble, a smash and a faint speck of ash,
One child's finger, foot and nose.
The people stood still, not daring to breathe,
With an almighty bang the hill became death,
Cloaked in black.
The people were screaming, dying and scared,
The children were crying,
The adults were scared.
The end of Pompeii was drawing near,
The ash, the fire and the death rained down.
That day Satan had his hands full,
With souls ripped slowly
From their casings and sent their separate way,
Some up and some down.

Alex Dennis (14)
Thomas Keble School

FIREWORKS

F ireworks set off in the dead of night,
I nspired by dribbles of colour,
R eactions are high with applause and cheering,
E nthusiasm rushes through the crowd,
W hispers when silence strikes
O verhead no movements made,
R ushes towards the - then *bang!*
K nowing what will become
S tar-scattered sky with flashes and sparks.

Rebecca Cook (11)
Thomas Keble School

My Brother's Work

My brother's work
He really loves
Is selling fish
And turtle doves.

With long, hard hours
And real good pay
The saying is
'All work, no play'.

The bet each week
Is to see who can
Trick someone
Like a silly old man.

The time is done
And the money's in
The doors are shut
'I've done the bun'.

We're in our cars
And on our way home
See you tomorrow
We all sadly moan.

Another hard day
We all have to do
We all earn a living
It's what we all do.

Kerrie Shaylor (14)
Thomas Keble School

WHAT IS WORK?

Work.
A strange word.
But what does it mean?
Does it mean going out every day to the same boring job?
Does it mean going to school and 'learning'?
Does it mean doing annoying jobs for your parents?
It could mean any of these,
Or it could mean:
Doing jobs to make money.
Going to school to get qualifications, to get jobs, to get money.
Or doing something to get you out of your house so you don't go mad!
Work.
A strange word.
And now you know what it means.

Samantha Jones (14)
Thomas Keble School

CAT

Witch's apprentice
Mice tracker
Vet hater
Bird chaser.

Dog fearer
Endless sleeper
Cuddle lover
Attention seeker.

Tail chaser
Loud purrer
Toy player
Flea bed.

Dainty paws
Water hater
Fish watcher
'Cat.'

Rachel Rendell (12)
Thomas Keble School

SONNET 666

Monsters hang out in your room ev'ry night,
You get monsters in all shapes and sizes,
They're multicoloured, some black, blue and white,
In ugly contests they would win prizes.

Monsters may be hiding under your bed
In your wardrobe, cupboard or chest of drawers,
In a corner or behind your bed head
They can break and enter and they have no laws.

What do they get up to while you're asleep?
Many monstrous, terrible things,
If you don't want nightmares you should not peep,
It leaves memories that tend to cling.

My advice to you is to check your room,
Beware of monsters when ent'ring the gloom.

Ysobel Baker (13)
Thomas Keble School

THE PIG POEM

Pigs live on farms,
and they sleep in barns,
some are made into bacon or ham,
they don't taste good if they're cooked with lamb.

Pigs eat pig food,
sometimes they get in a bad mood,
sometimes their tempers are high,
especially when they're about to be made into a pie.

Pigs are not known to kiss,
and if they do they're in bliss,
they have lots of babies,
some turn into pig ladies.

Pigs are a bore,
and they're not known to be good on a tour,
pigs are weird,
but they're not to be feared.

Sometimes they have a fever,
in the past they had a fight with a beaver,
pigs are pink,
and they can think.

Gabriel Raeburn (11)
Thomas Keble School

WHAT IS WORK?

When I was young, I would often say,
'Mum, what is work? Is it just like play?'
'No my dear,' would come the reply,
'Just do well at school and you'll soon see why.'
What was she saying? 'Do well' at school?

So work hard I did, I was nobody's fool.
Here I sit at my place of work,
I'll tell you something, you must not shirk.
Work can be hard, work can be cool,
But now I am somebody's fool.

Jenna Chudley (15)
Thomas Keble School

YOU'RE THE ADULT, I'M THE CHILD!

You're the adult, I'm the child
you are wise and I am wild.

You are tall and I am small
your mobile phone drives me up the wall.

You are right, I am wrong
but you and I like a little sing-song.

You go to bed early, I go to bed late,
but both of us like chocolate.

Your eyes are blue, mine are too,
sometimes you say I belong in the zoo.

You are sensible and I am mad,
you can be good and I can be bad.

You hate work and I hate school
because they are so *not* cool.

You like to watch TV and I like to play,
if we had the time we would do them all day.

You're the adult and I am the child,
you are wise and I am wild.

Ben Scrivens (13)
Thomas Keble School

A Keeper's Acrostic Poem

A crobatic save, as he tips the ball over the bar,
R unning up to take the corner,
T apping the ball into the open goal.
H appy winning the cup, not the first time,
U ncertain, he leaps into the air and catches the ball,
R acing off his goal line to grab the ball from the opponent's feet.

M urmuring crowd as he pulls off a great save,
I lluminated teams are rubbish, not us,
L eaping across the goal and catching the ball,
R aincloud overhead and we're getting worried,
O utrageous goalkeeping from the other team,
Y apping at his defence, he walks away.

Arthur Milroy (11)
Thomas Keble School

Work

Painting the house or fencing the garden,
It's work no matter which is harder.
Tiling the bathroom or fitting a tap,
Squeezing the filler into the gap.

Hoovering the carpet or dusting the wood,
A housewife does whatever she should.
Washing the floor and sweeping the mat,
Checking the hat stand and its hat.

It all contributes to the home,
Even the outside garden gnome.
Everyone has to work day or night,
Even on their home to get it right.

Emily Mayo (14)
Thomas Keble School

THE SEA

The sea is full of animals,
Animals bath in the sea, like otters,
Otters wrap themselves in seaweed and sleep.
Sleeping sea anemones wake when a diver goes past,
Past the rocks are the singing blue whales,
Whales with their calves go to feed,
Feeding on the flashing fish,
Fish come in big, small, colourful and dull.
Dull, it is not, in the sea always a good moment,
Moment the jet skis go past, animals fear,
Fear is the one bad thing in the sea pollution and people,
People catch fish, lobsters, even whales and dolphins.
Dolphins jump, always happy and graceful,
Graceful is the sea, never disturb the sea,
Sea will die without you.
You won't kill the sea, will you?

Amy Finch (12)
Thomas Keble School

INFINITY, ETERNITY, WORK

Infinity:
The eternity of numbers.

Eternity:
The work of life.

Life:
The infinity of work.

Laurence King (14)
Thomas Keble School

SONNET 1200

The roaring flames falling down from the sky,
The aroma of damp dew all around,
Falling, falling from the sky, saying, 'Bye,'
Different types of noises and sounds
Early morning smells set the day,
Feeling the coldness desiring pleasure,
Morning like evening like early May,
However the feeling cannot take measure,
Hundreds of colours coming at you
And in old woods, by chance, had seen,
Golden and yellow trees all around too,
Through fields and countries it has been,
As night came down the next day looked like rain,
But in the morning it repeats again.

Samantha Barclay (13)
Thomas Keble School

WORK

Work is hard, long and boring,
All I feel like is sitting and yawning.
When teacher's at the front talking and speaking,
All I feel like is sitting and sleeping.
Work can be fun,
But this is rare,
And when it is,
It gives me a scare.

Matt Saunders (15)
Thomas Keble School

CONSERVATION WORK

I stand before the congregation, slowly sinking into the dirt,
Solemn raindrops land.
I am armed with blades to slay the evil beasts, 'the nettles',
They sway in the distance, mocking me.

Last adjustments to my protective armour commence.
Lashing at me with their many arms,
These overgrown monsters live up to their ferocious reputation.

My flesh-tearing tools
Hack through their middles,
Clean in two,
Green blood spurts.

Kate Gaskell (14)
Thomas Keble School

FOOTBALL RIOT

Fast mover
Referee chaser
Goal swinger
Head bashers
Player beater
Naked streaker
Blood bringer
Coin thrower
Abuse user

Fence breaker
Seat smasher
Police fighters
Mouth gobber
Litter flicker
Chanting muncher
Bruised bumper
Knife slasher
Ball snatcher.

Dean Turner (12)
Thomas Keble School

MY TEACHER

I idolised my teacher,
She has travelled the world
Beaten illnesses you couldn't imagine,
She was superb.

I wanted to be like her,
I turned to her if I was bullied,
I turned to her if there was a problem,
I turned to her for comfort.

Her life was jam-packed with adventures,
She had seen everything,
Been to everything,
She was like a busybody wanting to do it all.

I grew older and my time at
Secondary school was near ending,
I didn't want to go, leave,
I wanted to stay.

But the teacher I adored was away from school,
She was nowhere in sight,
I asked teachers; but they would not tell,
Then I knew; she had a life-threatening illness.

I visited her every other week,
With flowers of all colours,
There would be other flowers too,
But not as colourful as mine.

I would sit for hours on end talking to her,
I even heard her voice like an echo
Telling me what I should do.
That phase has never worn.

Then my day arrived,
I travelled the world,
I was a teacher,
I was her!

Sophie Whitfield (13)
Thomas Keble School

LIFE IS FOREVER GOING

L ife is unfair,
I t's sometimes a dare,
F unny in ways,
E ven in days.

I s also Hell,
S ome memories ring a bell.

F orever going
O ver without knowing,
R eal sometimes,
E ven some crimes,
V ery cool,
E ven sometimes school
R eally fun.

G et good jobs done
O r it's a toy,
I t's sometimes joy.
N othing stops,
G ot lots and lots.

Saffa McGlynn (12)
Thomas Keble School

KENNING

Snow padder
Mist dweller
Steam breather
Ice melter.

Night walker
Wild crier
Fast trotter
Far howler.

Feared killer
Evil diner
Hungry threat
Vampire form.

Teeth barer
Cute creature
Noble hunter . . .

Canis Lupus.

Robbie Gillett (12)
Thomas Keble School

HAIKUS

Straw'bry jam is made
by squashing real strawberries,
it's quite good on toast.

I ate mouldy cheese,
with good rotten cucumber,
this was my nice lunch.

Andrew Roberts (11)
Thomas Keble School

FOOTBALL PLAYER

Hard tackler
Ball beater
Goal scorer
Ref arguer
Supporter autographer
Red carder
Flash cars
Big house
Training fanatic
Football tennis
Fit defender
Kick up champ.

Footio.

Matt Hobbs (12)
Thomas Keble School

CHRISTMAS

C hristmas trees are delivered to everyone's house
H appy faces when presents are opened
R eindeer's bells can be heard from the night sky
I n Father Christmas' sack there are hundreds of presents
S now falls on the ground where the children are playing
T oddlers are playing with their new presents
M ums and dads are filming their kids pulling the crackers
A snowman stands in the snow with its carrot nose
S oon after all the fun, the snow melts and the sun shines.

Peter Dempsey (13)
Thomas Keble School

FERRARI STREET RACER

Licence breaker,
Bone shaker.

Life taker,
No breaker.

Beating cars,
No superstars.

Kicking ass,
No driving on the grass.

Cops on tail,
Leaving a trail.

Getting in jail,
Allowed out on bail.

Simon Whiting (12)
Thomas Keble School

WHAT TO CALL A DOLPHIN

Water swisher
Fast swimmer
Cheeky squeaker
Blue rubber
Fast wriggler
Cheeky chap
Wave leaper
Smooth traveller
Deep sea diver.

Becky Hathaway (12)
Thomas Keble School

WHAT TO CALL MY DOG, JESSIE

Ball feather
Stick collector
Food backer
Water lapper
Loves walks
Can't talk
Black brother
Long-legged mother
Pheasant stalker
Quick walker
Fast runner
Bone lover
Man's best friend
Will never end.

Kate Carpenter (12)
Thomas Keble School

THE MOON

The moon is nice and bright.
Have a new adventure
Under the craters.
The moon is the heart of space.
The stars are the moon's soldiers
Protecting it all night.
The sun is the moon's enemy
It makes it go away!
I really love the moon.

Richard Hendy (14)
Thomas Keble School

It Ain't What You Do It's What It Does To You

I haven't walked through the Sahara
with only the last couple of drops of water
left,
I have sat on a Cornish beach
with ice cream dripping down my hand.

I haven't been scuba-diving
in a sea of coral,
I have swum at my local pool
with my friends.

I didn't go to Egypt
to see the pyramids,
I did go to Gloucester
to watch a film.

I wouldn't climb Everest
ever,
I do walk home
from the bus stop.

I haven't run in the Olympics
with the crowd cheering me on,
I have run the 1500 metres
round the school field.

Alex Hill (15)
Thomas Keble School

Monkey

Tree climber
Banana eater
Jungle squeaker
Tail swinger.

Furry friend
Cheeky chum
Branch hanger
Nutty creature.

Naomi Nobes (12)
Thomas Keble School

LATE NIGHT DOWN MONDAY CLOSE

A white cat walking down the back alley
She stops and hisses at the dog behind the fence.

A teenage boy comes by on a bike and scares the cat
He stops and laughs then sets off again.

An old man with a bushy beard and wrinkly skin is sitting in a bush
                                                         drinking from a bottle
He looks up and stares excitedly towards the sky.

The middle-aged family man across the road comes home at 8pm
He opens the car then locks it again and walks inside.

At 10pm or 11pm the bikers rev their engines to start a foolish race
They go past once or twice and then stop.

I look out of the window and see them laughing
They hold up a piece of paper that's on fire.

A siren starts, the bikers scatter everywhere
The movement was not needed as the car flies past.

Then all the birds sing their morning tunes and
It starts all over again.

James Hemming (13)
Thomas Keble School

THE HORSE

Angry bucker
Stable mucker
Clippy clopper
Foal protector
Dreamy starer
Bucket slurper
Tail swisher
Fly swatter
People carrier
Hard worker
Eager competitor
Lofty jumper
Steeple chaser
Rapid racer
Saddle wearer
Hay muncher
Hoof stamper
Equus.

Kate Espley (12)
Thomas Keble School

A CAT

Milk drinker
Mouse chaser
Friendly feline
Lazy creature.

Speedy eater
Funny preacher
Street fighter
Big time beater.

Flea carrier
Milk lapper
All day sleeper
Fat feline.

Craig Banyard (12)
Thomas Keble School

IT AIN'T WHAT YOU DO BUT WHAT IT DOES TO YOU

I have not been on a spree in New York
With £10,000 to spare in Ralph Lauren,
Bloomindales and Macey's,
I have been shopping in Stroud.

I have not been to The Ivy,
The restaurant where the stars go,
Escargot and Chateaubriand,
I have been to McDonald's.

I have not been on the London Eye
Gazing at the city around,
The ant-like people and Big Ben,
I have been on the biscuit tin at the fair.

I have not lived on my own
In my own apartment, doing whatever I please,
Dressing how I like and music full-blast,
I have lived with my gran.

I have not done some of the greatest things,
But I have done the small things that count!

Becki Short (15)
Thomas Keble School

WHAT TO CALL A PUPPY

Food gobblers
      Quick growlers
Sound sleepers
      Fast runners
Ball chasers
      Rule breakers
Fun makers
      Heart takers
Curious sniffers
      Clumsy walkers
Sloppy lickers
      High whiners
Noisy barkers
      Nosy parkers.

Canis.

Alice Crick (12)
Thomas Keble School

DOG

Tail wagger
Cat scrapper
Food eater
Lead partner.

Loud barker
Wall marker
Book eater
Toy beater.

Bird chaser
Heart breaker
Nose wetter
Noise maker.

Bone chomper
Vet hater
Plant wrecker
Walk lover.
Canis.

Laura Northcott (12)
Thomas Keble School

CAT

Milk drinker,
Long sleeper,
Flea scratcher,
Fast runner,
Mouse catcher,
Food eater,
Quiet sneaker,
Ball chaser,
High jumper,
Dog fearer,
Tree climber,
Bird taker,
Cattus.

Paul Stephens (12)
Thomas Keble School

WHAT AM I?

Sky soarer
Fast flyer
Droppings dropper
Grub grabber
Great glider
Worm wrestler
Feather brain
Streamline scorcher
Dive bomber
Glossy coating.

What am I?

I'm a bird.

James Westerby (12)
Thomas Keble School

KENNING: A DOG

Cat hater
Bird grabber
Tail chaser
Bottom smeller.

Lead puller
Fast walker
Race runner
Walk lover.

Puddle licker
Water slurper
Loud barker
Vet hater.

Jamie Ponting (12)
Thomas Keble School

MY FATHER

My father grasped the jet-black gel pen
between his fingers.
I looked down at the sky-blue textbook,
confusion filled my empty mind.

My father sped up suddenly,
the English questions faded from the page
As they were depleted, one by one,
from the sky-blue textbook.

I looked up at him through tears of
admiration.
His abilities seemed limitless, as though he knew everything
needing known in this obtuse world.

My gaze returned to the textbook,
from which my tears had begun.
I looked for a clue or sign of my
father's intelligence, but I found nothing.

Trying to find the source of his mind
was like trying to grab hold of a handful of mist.
My mind exploded, my ears burst and
my vision seemed to fail.

Now, however, I understand how my father
had become so smart.
He had grown up into the man known as
my father.

I look at my textbook now and smile;
I see the answers appear on the page.
The answer to my original question is now the easiest of all
to answer: He had grown up.

Grant Tudor (13)
Thomas Keble School

IT AIN'T WHAT YOU DO, IT'S WHAT IT DOES TO YOU

I have not swum with dolphins
In the deep blue Mediterranean Sea
But I have been swimming with my friends
At Stroud Leisure Centre.

I have not watched my favourite band live
At a concert
But I have watched my two cousins
Perform in a talent contest.

I have not lived in Buckingham Palace
But I have been to Sleeping Beauty's Palace in Disneyworld.

I have not been parachuting
Instead I have kept my feet firmly on the floor
While watching someone else do it.

Sadie Whiting (15)
Thomas Keble School

WHAT AM I?

Wind catcher
Water slicer
Fish scarer
Damp maker.

Hair whipper
Water sprayer
Weed tickler
Smooth sailor.

Sky starer
Race winner
Person carrier
Ailingsay Oatbay

Rebecca Starkiss (12)
Thomas Keble School

IT AIN'T WHAT YOU DO, IT'S WHAT IT DOES TO YOU

I have not cruised the world
On sun-soaked oceans
But I have boated down a Somerset canal
With my uncle on a crisp autumn evening.

I haven't visited Hollywood
And met the movie stars in all their glory
But I have gone to the local cinema
On a rainy Sunday and entered another world.

I have not tackled Hawaii waves on
A lemon-yellow, waxed-down surfboard
But I have braved the pebble-swarming seas of a
Cornwall beach on a summer holiday.

I have not attempted Formula 1 driving
Alongside Damon Hill on a twisted Japanese racetrack,
But I have go-karted with my little cousin
And supported him before the big race!

And, I believe, the heart-stopping tension, and that
Cascading emotion somewhere inside of me
Is part of a sense of something else. That feeling, you know.

Michael Eedle (16)
Thomas Keble School

A LONELY MAN

Walking along a cold, lonely road,
I stumble across all kinds of things,
But this wasn't right, this never happened,
I wasn't prepared for this experience.
I didn't usually walk down this street,
It was tranquil and depressing, just grey, hard walls.
Homeless people with no friends, no life, just a blanket for warmth
                                                                     at night,

Some things are miracles, some are fate,
But I couldn't figure this one out,
Why did I see him, why did we meet?
One split second, how can I learn so much from one glimpse?

His eye is bloodshot, from sleepless nights on a hard, dreary floor,
His inside's full of hurt and shattered dreams,
A smart brain full of life and cells,
Wasted on naivety and being too trustworthy.
A torn, tatty shirt his only form of clothing,
His calm, blue, tranquil pools that are his eyes, the windows to his soul.
However, through the windows there is a scene of anger and hate,
No sign from the outside, but inside is just revenge and hatred,
Frantic movement and a vigorous rush,
These signs mean some kind of argument,
An argument? It seemed more like a boxing match.

Through his eyes pieces of paper are being flung around in a
                                                      whirlpool of madness,
Two men's mouths are moving with evil in their voices,
But for some reason the mute is on.
In a gush of pent-up emotion a computer is hurled,
No one is hurt but it's clear someone's finished when the boss walks in.
The lonely man walks out in disgrace,
He cannot find work and can't pay his bills.

With no place to go, he ends up on the street,
But some things trouble me,
What was the argument about? What were they saying and did he
have a family?

Goodbye lonely man.

Ben Payne (13)
Thomas Keble School

IT AIN'T WHAT YOU DO, IT'S WHAT IT DOES TO YOU

I have not journeyed through the Amazon,
marvelling at the wonderful scenery;
but I have been camping in Cornwall
in a tent that leaked in the pouring rain.

I have not parachuted from a plane
and watched the ground rise up to meet me;
but I have sat in an exam, knowing
that I have not revised enough for it.

I have not travelled across the Sahara
riding a camel in the oppressive heat;
but I have sat on a beach in Exmouth,
hot sand blowing in my face, burning me.

I have not been to the freezing North Pole,
numb with the biting cold, covered in snow;
but I have walked to school on a frosty morning
with a bag full of books, weighing a ton.

But I guess that the feelings from what I have done
are just as valuable as the more exciting things
people have done in life.
Those feelings, that sense of something else.

Jenny Warner (15)
Thomas Keble School

WHAT YOU HAD AND WHEN IT'S GONE

You never realise what you had,
Until it's actually gone.
I understand what I said
And regret the things I've done.

If only the clocks could be turned back,
I do not doubt I'd change.
All the bad that should have been good,
I'd make them all the same.

It's hard to get on with everyday life,
Knowing what you had,
Facing all the facts there are,
Makes one really sad.

The light's gone out, I'm left in the dark,
I will think of this till I die.
What I had and now it's gone,
Makes me want to cry.

Holly Brown (15)
Thomas Keble School

AFRAID

I too, have been afraid
Have stayed in bed and dreamed of freedom.
Now I am afraid of the wind singing my name
I have no option but to be brave.
The rain tapping on the window asking me to come out.

Matthew Flagg (15)
Thomas Keble School

IT AIN'T WHAT YOU DO, IT'S WHAT IT DOES TO YOU

I have not lived in San Francisco in a local drug den,
I have lived my life in Stroud with peer pressure at my side.

I did not marry a famous actor, like Brad Pitt, as a rich and active wife,
But I have lived my life in a boring sequence, up at seven, bed at night.

I have never toyed with £10,000 as I spend my way through New York,
I have padded my way through Tesco's on a dull Saturday morning
                                                          buying the usual dairy.

I have not been in a brilliant catwalk show as a famous supermodel,
I have taken part in my local pantomime.

And I guess everyone does something in their lives as radical as these,
But have they lived a life of me?
That's what I mean . . .

Emily Coles (15)
Thomas Keble School